VICTORIAN
LAKELAND PHOTOGRAPHERS

Stephen F. Kelly

SWAN·HILL
PRESS

DEDICATION
For my mother

First published in the UK in 1991 by
Swan Hill Press

British Library Cataloguing in Publication Data
    Kelly, Stephen
    Victorian lakeland photographers.
    1. Cumbria (England). Photography. History
    I. Title
    770.232094278
    ISBN 1 85310 233 4

Printed in England by Livesey Ltd., Shrewsbury.

Swan Hill Press
An Imprint of Airlife Publishing Ltd.
101 Longden Road, Shrewsbury SY3 9EB, England.

CONTENTS

ACKNOWLEDGEMENTS

This book was born in a Keswick restaurant one Saturday evening. On the walls were a number of Victorian photographs, one of which particularly caught my eye. It was of a stout bowler-hatted gentleman proudly displaying the salmon he had just netted. I eventually persuaded the restaurant owner to sell me the photograph and to this day it adorns a wall of my house. And there began a tale. It transpired that when work had begun on the restaurant a few years previously a stack of dusty old glass plate negatives had been unearthed in the loft. A little research revealed that the premises had once been the studio of Henry Mayson, the celebrated Keswick photographer. The plates were cleaned up and the results were there on display in the restaurant which had also been appropriately named after him.

So, in the first place my thanks to Robin Bainbridge, the owner of Mayson's Restaurant, for selling me the photograph and initiating this idea. In particular however I would especially like to thank John Marsh of the Abbot Hall Museum in Kendal who has encouraged this venture since its inception, guiding me through the maze of Lakeland photographers and patiently helping wherever was possible. I should also like to thank Vicky Slowe and the staff of Abbot Hall, including Janet Dugdale and Philip Dalziel for all their generous help as well as for permission to copy many of the glass plates in their extensive collection. Thanks also to the Fell and Rock Climbing Club who similarly allowed me to borrow the original glass plate negatives of the Abraham collection. Christine Strickland at the Kendal Library also deserves special mention as does Peter McIntyre and the Armitt Trust in Ambleside who generously allowed me to borrow from their archives. My appreciation also to the staff at Windermere and Keswick libraries.

Mention should also be given to Harry Fancy at Whitehaven Museum who tried in vain to find glass plates and information on James Bellman; Janet Baker at the Helena Thompson Museum in Workington who repeatedly disappeared into the vaults to return with more photographs from their W. C. Lawrie collection; and Miss Gaddes at Lancaster library whose appreciation of Sam Thompson deserves special applause. I am also grateful to Reg Dixon who allowed me to borrow his Baldry plates and David Scott who gave vital biographical information on William Baldry. Raymond Sankey also provided prints from his father's extensive collection as well as biographical details while George Holt of Keswick provided me with some of his Mayson photographs. Thanks also to the Wordsworth Trust at Grasmere, the Royal Photographic Society who kindly sifted their files and Michael Harvey at the National Museum of Photography in Bradford who similarly examined their archives and gave much-needed advice on the technical aspects of early photography. If there are any mistakes, they are mine alone.

Many others gave valuable help including Liz Andrew, Nigel Lord, Betty Fagg, George Bott, Hilary Gray of *Cumbria* magazine, Alan Monkhouse, the Kendal Public Records Office, Margaret Russell of the Cumbria Family History Society, Geoffrey Thompson, Alan Hankinson and Michael Moon.

A special word of appreciation should be given to John Broughton of the Grange Photographic Society who so patiently and expertly developed the bulk of photographs in this book from the original glass plate negatives. My publishers also should be acknowledged for the faith which they placed in this project, especially Alastair Simpson and my editor John Beaton who were as encouraging and helpful as possible as was my agent John Pawsey. Finally, special thanks to my wife Judith, Nicholas and Emma who never grew weary of my trips to the Lakes and who supported this idea from that very first evening long ago at Mayson's Restaurant in Keswick.

Stephen F. Kelly
Manchester, 1991

INTRODUCTION

The Lake District was not always the delight it is today. There was a time when visitors scorned its craggy mountains and gloomy landscape. When the writer Daniel Defoe travelled its length and breadth in 1722 he was barely impressed describing the countryside as 'the wildest, most barren and frightful of any that I have past over in England, or even in Wales'. Not even the majestic Great Gable or the Langdale Pikes held much appeal for him. The mountains had 'a kind of unhospitable terror in them . . . all barren and wild, of no use or advantage to man or beast,' he wrote as he journeyed.

Yet we should hardly be surprised at Defoe's comments. In eighteenth century England the Lake District must have appeared a miserable, damp and unfriendly spot. Roads were few and far between and always impassable in winter while the twenty mile journey from Windermere to Keswick would have taken up the best part of a day. Even in 1890 it took as long as three hours by coach on what was arguably the best road in the Lakes, even then little short of a rough track. 'I had rather travel from Maine to Georgia by rail, than from Grasmere to Windermere by stage-coach, wrote the American novelist Nathaniel Hawthorne after a hazardous visit to the Lakes in 1855.

Away from the main routes the roads were mere stony paths. Villages and hamlets were isolated; people rarely ventured beyond their village boundaries and never further than a dozen or so miles which was usually done either on foot or by horse. Indeed it was not uncommon for people to walk as much as forty miles in a day. It was not an easy life. Houses were damp and bitterly cold during the invariably harsh winters. There was no central heating, no hot water, gas or electricity. All the modern components which make life in the Lake District so bearable and enjoyable today were sadly lacking. There was no jumping into the car to drive to the nearest supermarket or into Kendal for any last minute shopping. There was little in the way of entertainment. No theatres, cinemas, television, radio, or videos. It was usually the local inn or nothing and even that was a male preserve.

The women remained at home, cooking, looking after the house and rearing as many as a dozen children. Some congregated around the church which, like the inn, was often the focal point of the village community.

Along with Defoe, the artists were also setting the scene with their gloomy and depressing paintings. Charles Towne, Julius Caesar Ibbetson and Philip James de Louterbourg had all ventured into the region and painted bleak canvases of swirling storms, and rising rivers. It was enough to discourage anyone from exploring the area. Travellers were few and far between, making the Lakes almost a closed community. A regular coach service did not commence until the early nineteenth century and only the most determined traveller stepped beyond Lancaster and Kendal. But all that changed with the poets who began to popularise the Lakes by presenting a different image. Wordsworth, Southey, Coleridge, Arnold, Ruskin and others discovered instead a splendour and majesty in its surrounds. 'A cabinet of beauties' was how Coleridge described it. For them the Lakes had a lyrical quality — lofty mountains, peaceful vales, warm forests and quiet fells. Their writings helped spread the news and paint a fresh picture of Lakeland life. The tourists were about to take up their call but not until the Industrial Revolution had ushered in the arrival of steam.

The railways were not initially welcomed in Lakeland. 'Weighing the mischief with the promised gain . . . I call on you to share the passion of a just disdain' wrote Wordsworth scathingly in 1844. But despite his opposition the railway still came with the first line linking London and Windermere opening in 1847. At the time Windermere was an insignificant hamlet with a population of no more than a few hundred and more popularly known as Birthwaite. But the coming of the railway changed all that. The station was named Windermere and the hamlet began to expand as the tourists poured out of their carriages and made their way down the road to the Lake where they would while away an hour or so on one of the Furness Railway's steamers or simply admire the tranquillity. The line ended here and although proposals to extend it to Ambleside were planned, the project was eventually shelved. It was technically difficult and there was considerable opposition to the idea, particularly from Canon Rawnsley (later to become founder of the National Trust). It would be a further twenty-seven years before the northern lakes enjoyed the benefit of steam and then they were linked with Penrith in the east rather than with the southern Lake District towns of Grasmere or Ambleside.

Before long the railways began to bring tourists. Not many at first, merely the wealthy with time on their hands to explore and money in their pockets to spend. Later as industry introduced the six day week and regular holidays, the railways offered cheap excursions introducing the professional and middle classes to the area. Finally, the industrial workers of Lancashire, eventually released from their seven day a week jobs, took advantage of third class cheap day excursions. They came in their thousands, some staying for a week or so, but many simply visiting for the day, sailing on the lake or idling their precious hours around Windermere or Bowness.

Just as the first railways were arriving in Lakeland, so William Henry Fox Talbot's early experiments with photography began to pay dividends. The photographic revolution was set to explode. By the 1850s the camera had even arrived as far north as the Lake District with the first known photograph taken in 1852 of John Marsden, a customs officer. By 1858 *Kelly's Trade Directory* was listing two professional photographers in the area. They were Joseph Fletcher at Bowness and George Waters at Windermere. Nothing is known of Fletcher and none of his photographs seem to have survived but thankfully we do know a little about George Waters. By 1869 he had transferred his operation a mile down the road to Bowness where most of the tourists tended to congregate, converging on the lake and its pleasure steamers. We also know that by the 1880s Waters had installed a relief model of the Lakes in his Bowness Gallery, similar to the one constructed by Joseph Flintoft in Keswick. But unlike Flintoft, Waters had built his model after the release of the ordnance survey maps and had not had to trek the length and breadth of the Lakes measuring every mile.

In common with many photographers of the time Waters also displayed a wide range of paintings in his studio and at one time even ran an ironmonger's shop. Sadly, only a handful of his photographs have survived the years and there now appear to be no glass plates in existence. Yet from the few prints that do exist it is clear that he possessed an exceptional talent. There are magnificent stills of anglers idling their time away on quiet backwaters and boats gently lying on restful lakes. Of all the Lakeland photographers Waters, who died in 1935, is undoubtedly the most romantic. Largely forgotten, he is perhaps more entitled to be recognised as the father of Lakeland photography than even Alfred Pettitt of Keswick who is usually bestowed with the honour.

George Waters was almost certainly the first commercial photographer in the Lakes. He had opened a studio in Windermere prior to 1858 but later moved to Bowness. This etching of his Bowness studio, made in 1885, shows the growing attraction of relief models.

The *Kelly's Directory* of 1869 listed eleven photographers in Cumberland and Westmorland. Three of those were in Whitehaven, three in Keswick, two in Ambleside, two in Bowness and one in Grasmere. The revolution was under way; four years later the list had expanded to almost thirty throughout the two counties with sixteen of those operating in the Lakes. Many of them concentrated on studio work and their collections have long since disappeared without trace while others have left a few memories and just a handful have left substantial portfolios. We shall never, for instance, know about Moses Bowness who trained a number of fine Lakeland photographers, nor about the quality of James Sproat's work, nor about Thomas Irving of Cockermouth.

Once the photographic industry was under way competition began to emerge. There was not always enough work and three or four photographers operating in the same town was sometimes one too many. The result was

Few photographs by George Waters have survived the years but this peaceful fishing scene taken in 1880 surely ranks among the finest by any of the Victorian Lakeland photographers.

intense rivalry. It first manifested itself over Joseph Flintoft's famous scale model of the Lakes which had been an enormous attraction. It was on view in Keswick Town Hall daily for a small admission charge. Flintoft was a Yorkshireman who had come to the Lakes to partake of the hunting and fishing but somehow or other had become obsessed with making a relief model of the area. At this time it should be remembered there were no Ordnance Survey maps and to gauge his model Flintoft

trekked the fells and peaks of the two counties, measuring each mile and the altitude of every mountain. It was an enormous undertaking which took more than seven years to complete but in the end he proudly boasted a superb model on a scale of three inches to the mile. It was exhibited in the Town Hall and was listed as a star attraction in all the guidebooks.

On rainy days Flintoft's model was the obvious port of call for tourists. Quite whether the undertaking was financially worth seven years exertion we shall never know but it certainly tempted others to construct similar models. And for some reason it was the photographers who followed his example. Perhaps they saw it as a means of supplementing their income or of drawing customers to their premises where they could then tempt them to pose for a family portrait. Whatever the reason the photographic studios soon became a focal point for the tourist, a sort of Victorian fun palace where they could browse, looking at the oil paintings or admire the photographic landscapes as well as the scale models. George Waters built one for his Bowness studio while up in Keswick Henry Mayson, and later George Abraham, also built models, though on a much larger scale than Flintoft's. The latter again having the advantage of the newly published ordnance survey maps which made them a more economically viable proposition.

Photography was still primarily studio based where it was technically easier and more financially rewarding. In the late nineteenth century having your photograph taken was not a cheap indulgence and it was usually the middle classes to be found posing in front of the camera. A special event such as a wedding or christening might widen the social range of customers but for the average family such occasions were few and far between. There were also added difficulties in photographing outdoors as this meant carting a considerable amount of equipment around. When Roger Fenton made his famed tours he travelled with a horsedrawn van; others had collapsible tents though in time portable dark tents would be manufactured making life a little easier. Nor was there much call for landscape photography, especially in the Lake District where paintings were still considered the vogue. It would not be until the emergence of the picture postcard industry later in the century that landscape photography began to flourish.

The coming of the railway was to dramatically reshape the Lake District. It would no longer be a self-contained community, cut-off from the rest of the nation but was about to become a tourist centre. A further boost to tourism came with the introduction of paid holidays during the latter part of the nineteenth century. Prior to 1860 workers were lucky to be given a couple of day's leave a year but by the end of the century industrial workers across a whole range of industry had won further concessions. More than half a million railway workers for instance in 1897 secured an agreement giving them an eight hour day and a week's holiday with pay while cotton workers in Lancashire had won similar conditions

The Abraham Brothers, perhaps the most famous of all Lakeland photographers, whose mountaineering photographs pioneered a new dimension in photography.

before the century was over. Both these industries were important to the development of tourism in the Lakes. Railway workers had special travel privileges and could travel to the Lakes with their families for a fraction of the normal cost. Lancashire cotton workers, and there were well over 600,000 of them, although not paid sufficient to take a week's holiday in the Lakes were located close enough to be able to afford a day trip.

Tourism was on the march, or more appropriately, on the railway. It cost little to travel by train and the L & NW Railway Company introduced cheap day excursions and third class rail fares to entice industrial workers to the resorts and countryside. A third class return from London to Windermere cost just under £2, while from Manchester it was a mere twelve shillings (60p). And mostly it was from Lancashire that they came, travelling in their thousands from Manchester, Liverpool, Bolton, Preston, Lancaster, Bury and Blackpool. Those coming from

A typical Abraham photograph. This is a simple but dramatic landscape of Wasdale Head and Wastwater taken from the upper reaches of Great Gable. Creating this shot meant carting camera, chemicals, dark room, and tripod up the mountainside.

13

Blackpool usually arrived in the early morning by pleasure steamer from Fleetwood and then took the short hop on the railway to Windermere. There they would spend the day before catching an early evening train back to Barrow, and then the boat to Fleetwood, arriving back at their B and B's just in time for their evening meal.

Holidaymakers meant postcards. A cheap and efficient mail service was already operating by the 1890s, partly encouraged by the success of the postcard which had proved to be an inexpensive and simple form of correspondence. The postcard had been introduced to the world in Austria in 1869 and the Abraham Brothers, on a visit to Switzerland, were among the first to realise its potential. There they had bought scenic postcards to send home to their family and friends in the Keswick area. When they returned it was with the idea of purchasing new premises and printing their own cards for the holidaymakers now descending on the Lakes. Others quickly followed suit although most either had their postcards printed elsewhere or simply sold their picture to a major manufacturer such as Valentines or Raphael Tucks. The cards were cheap and within reach of anyone's pocket. By 1900 it was a prospering business giving a major fillip to the photographic industry.

The postcard industry quickly led to further rivalry. At first customers were quite content with simple street scenes of Ambleside or Windermere but they soon became bored and demanded better. The summery landscape, photographed from the highest fell, became the fashion and the photographers were forced to pick up their equipment and clamber up the peaks to capture more expansive scenes. Then the Abraham Brothers went one better with their winter landscapes forcing others to take their cameras and tripods into the wintery frozen wastes. The Abrahams were trend setters and before long they were producing dramatic mountaineering shots which did a brisk trade among the climbing fraternity. Few could rival their climbing photographs which even to this day rank among some of the finest ever taken.

Other photographers such as the Herbert Brothers offered a different approach by dividing their postcards into four squares so that four different shots could be shown. And often an oval shaped picture might also be decoratively placed in the middle, perhaps with a 'good luck' or 'greetings' motto. Then along came the folding postcard, a sort of concertina of eight or more pictures, which was more expensive but highly popular. It was all part of the emerging industry. Competition led to improvements in technique, design and picture quality.

But while the surge for more dramatic landscapes had the photographers chasing over the fells there was equal competition on the ground. The major events such as Queen Victoria's jubilees of 1887 and 1897, Kaiser Wilhelm's visit and the great freeze of 1895 found them competing with each other to capture the memorable occasion. When Windermere was frozen solid in February 1895 at least three photographers — William Brunskill, Robert Bell and Henry Herbert — joined the clamour on the ice.

Some photographers specialised. The Abraham Brothers became renowned for their mountaineering photographs while Henry Mayson preferred the quiet solitude of his studio. William Carruthers Lawrie of Workington, a lifelong ornithologist, excelled in bird photography while Edward Sankey delighted in photographing the many ships that slid down the slipways at Vickers shipyard in Barrow. It was usually the case that the more specialised you were, the greater your chance of survival.

Perhaps the greatest burden of the Victorian photographer was his equipment. No 35mm lightweight cameras with interchangeable lenses in those days. Instead, a heavy field or stand camera, usually made of mahogany with leather bellows and brass fittings. And for those who photographed outdoors using the wet collodion process, it was also necessary to have a tent as well as camera, tripod, chemicals, plate-holders, glass plates, dishes, glassware and a supply of water, all of which had to be lugged around, often by cart, but usually on the photographer's back. The burden was eased a little in 1862 when W. W. Rouch began manufacturing a portable dark tent which proved to be immensely popular. It included a small yellow window which allowed the photographer to see what he was doing along with pockets for the various chemicals and storage jars and a shelf on which the chemicals could be mixed.

The wet collodion technique had been introduced in 1851 by F. Scott Archer and was the principal method of photography until the 1880s. Indeed its high quality kept it in favour with many specialist photographers until well into the twentieth century. Basically a clean thin glass plate would be coated with a collodion solution containing potassium iodide. Then the plate would be immersed in the dark in a silver nitrate solution. The silver nitrate reacted with the potassium iodide to form light sensitive silver iodide or silver bromo-iodide. The wet plate would then be exposed and immediately afterwards processed before the collodion dried and became impervious to the solutions. The negative would then be fixed in a solution of potassium cyanide and washed. Finally, when dry, the plate would be given a protective covering of spirit varnish to preserve its qualities. It was a complicated, time consuming process which clearly required a dark-room on site and a store of chemicals. The total weight of all this baggage could come to anything between 30 and 100 pounds. But the results were usually worthwhile with high quality fine grain negatives that even to this day produce superb prints. This complicated use of chemicals led a number of artists to mockingly suggest that photography was merely a matter of chemicals. The photographer Roger Fenton fittingly replied to their accusation that 'in like manner as the painter is dependent on pencils, colours and canvas'.

The glass plates were also delicate and had to be carried in a special grooved box that held them tightly in place. Although enlargers were being manufactured by the late nineteenth century there was no simple method of enlargement and if you wanted a larger photograph you generally used a larger plate. The most popular size glass plate for exterior photography was 8½ x 6½ inches although smaller sizes were also popular, particularly with the amateur. Nor was it uncommon to see 20 x 16 inch plates or even larger being used, especially in the studio. Today it is hard to imagine anyone being inclined to trek up fells or climb mountains with so much equipment. Yet the Victorian cameraman had little altern-ative and seems hardly to have been deterred by the weight of his cumbersome load. And in the case of the Slingsby sisters of Grange — two frail old ladies — the burdensome weight seems not to have discouraged their ventures.

In 1871 the photographer's cargo was eased a little when Dr Richard Leach Maddox introduced the dry plate method which simplified the process and did away with much of the paraphernalia of the wet plate technique. But it would be a further ten years before the method became commercially popular. The advantage here was that the plate could be prepared in advance back in the studio. A glass plate would be coated with a gelatin emulsion instead of collodion to make the plate sensitive to the light. This was made by mixing melted gelatin with a halide such as silver nitrate. The plate was then dried and stored away until it was needed. Once the exposure had been taken the image on the plate could be processed at any time. It meant that photographers need only carry their plates and camera with them when they set off on an expedition up the fells. Adverts at the time even showed

women using the camera, just to illustrate how easy it had all become!

The most popular camera up until the late 1860s was the sliding box camera which would almost certainly have numbered in the stock of any of the professional Lakeland photographers. They were not cheap. In 1856 Lewis Carroll purchased one in London for £15. Although it was heavy and awkward to carry, a folding version with bellows was later developed along with a lens panel and plate holder that could be removed enabling the sides of the camera to be folded flat, making it more compact and easier to carry. Camera designs of course improved but up until the First World War most professional photographers would have clung to their hardy field cameras which, despite their bulk, produced superb results. Nor was there any easy method of measuring the light in order to calculate the exposure. Exposures were made simply by removing the lens cap, counting the calculated number of seconds and then replacing the cap. And because the exposure took a few seconds, it was also necessary to have a tripod. Knowing the necessary length of exposure time required considerable skill and experience on the part of the photographer and it is quite common in collections to find three or four attempts at the same subject, each using a different time exposure. Some photography magazines even produced tables to assist the cameraman and later still calculators were introduced. Built-in shutters, enabling exposures of less than one second did not appear until the 1880s and probably would not have been adopted by the Lakeland cameraman until the turn of the century.

The majority of landscape work would be taken on a simple achromatic lens with a maximum aperture of f.16 while studio portraits would more than likely be shot on a Petzal f.3.6 lens. Telephoto lenses were rarely used before 1900 and W. C. Lawrie, the bird photographer would have shot most of his photographs using a long focal length. Ironically, many of the more wealthy tourists who arrived in the Lakes during the last few years of the nineteenth century would have done so with their own cameras. In 1887 George Eastman revolutionised photo-graphy by introducing the Kodak roll film camera so that while the Lakeland photographers struggled behind their heavy field cameras the tourists were enjoying themselves with their small hand held Kodaks.

Wherever possible the photographs reproduced in this book have been printed directly from the original glass plate negatives. But sadly few have withstood the rigours of time and even those that have survived have often been

Little is known of William Brunskill and only a handful of his pictures have survived. But like many others Brunskill was on the ice at Windermere during the great freeze of February 1895 when the Lake was frozen from end to end.

The railway station at Grange-Over-Sands, then part of the Furness Railway as seen by Brunskill.

damaged by the damp or suffered chemical defects. In order to include some photographers we have had to resort to using prints which has inevitably led to a decline in quality. There have been other problems. Biographical information on many of the photographers is sketchy and consequently some outstanding candidates have been omitted. People like William Brunskill, the Bowness photographer should, and would, have been included had any of his glass plates survived. Unfortunately, all that remains today are a large collection of postcards and a small number of ageing prints which were rescued from a rubbish dump at the turn of the century by the Bowness shopkeeper Frank Robinson. Commonly known as Fenty, Robinson displayed the photographs in an album in his draper's shop and it soon became known as Fenty's Album. Today his albums are in the safe keeping of Windermere Library. To have taken further copies from these already decaying prints in the albums would have meant a decline in quality which would have done a disservice to his work.

A further problem has been in identifying the photographer. Occasionally prints may have been stamped but usually there is no means of identification unless they belong to a specified collection. In Fenty's album, for instance, there are many prints where the photographer cannot be pinpointed and could easily have been accredited to any number of Bowness or Windermere photographers.

Brunskill, whose photographs span the 1880s and 90s, worked in Bowness and was one of the first professional photographers on Windermere during the great freeze of February 1895 when the ten and a half mile long lake was frozen from end to end with eighteen inches of ice. It was a unique occasion that is still legendary in Lakeland history, thanks partly to the photographs of Brunskill and others. Nearby was 'photographic artist' George H. Brockbank whose studio in Windermere was established in 1899, and of course there was George Waters who pioneered the way for so many photographers working in the area as well as James Garnett who was established as a

17

photographer at the Post Office in Windermere as early as the 1860s. Like Brunskill they deserve recognition but lack of glass plates, and even prints, has led to their omission. Included however are the Herbert Brothers, perhaps the best known of the Bowness photographers whose studios were established in the 1880s and continued until long after the Second World War.

While Bowness was the centre in the south, Keswick was the headquarters of the north producing perhaps the most celebrated of all Lakeland photographers — the Abraham Brothers. But they were not alone. Alfred Pettitt and Henry Mayson also worked the northern fells before the turn of the century, each bringing a different interpretation to the way and life of the small market town. Another centre was the busy town of Kendal where James Henry Hogg had been associated with photography since 1858 along with William Moscrop and Thomas Rigg while in Ambleside there was Lovell Mason who with

his two brothers ran the 'Art Gallery' on what is still known as Mason's Corner. Mason also photographed the Grasmere Sports, in particular Cumberland wrestling and its most famous combatant, George Steadman. John Bankes was another photographer based in Ambleside where he took photographs for the Titus Wilson publication *Two Hundred Views of the English Lakes*, but the best known of all Ambleside photographers were Herbert Bell and Charles Walmsley, both of whom have fortunately left many examples of their work, some of which appear in the following pages. Up in Grasmere William Baldry after an early career as the local schoolmaster took to photography and not only helped set up the now famous Grasmere Sports but also became its official photographer. Baldry also recorded the construction of Thirlmere reservoir which brought so many topographical changes to the area.

While these were the photographers of the principal

Brunskill was one of the first Lakeland photographers to record everyday events such as this cattle auction. Taken around 1890 it was an occasion that clearly called for top hats and suits.

Lovell Mason of Ambleside took many photographs of the Grasmere Sports. This general view of the paddock was taken in 1907.

Mason was not averse to doctoring some of his photographs. At the time lenses had not been perfected to counter any blurring where there was movement. Yet Mason has clearly been at work here producing as sharp an action shot as you could expect from a modern camera.

Two famous Cumberland wrestlers, Hexham Clarke with his back to the camera and George Steadman. Steadman who died in 1904 won the heavyweight contest at the Grasmere Sports on fourteen occasions and is reckoned to be the greatest of all Cumberland wrestlers.

19

James Bellman the Whitehaven photographer is best known for his pictures of Whitehaven harbour and the Wellington Pit Disaster of 1910. These three photographs show sailing vessels in the harbour at Whitehaven.

Lakeland towns there were others on the fringes of the Lakes who equally deserve mention. At Whitehaven on the west coast of Cumbria James Bellman and Henry Roper were photographing sailing ships in the harbour and workers at the nearby Harrington shipyard during the 1870s. Sadly only a handful of their prints have survived and as far as is known there are no glass plates still in existence. Bellman was a particularly interesting photographer concentrating on the industrial life of the area rather than its landscape. Perhaps he was simply

reflecting the town he lived in but for the times it was a refreshing and innovative approach. His portfolio includes not only the shipyard and dockside workers of Whitehaven but miners as well. He was on hand at the Wellington pit disaster in May 1910 when 136 miners lost their lives and recorded the terrible scene with some poignant portraits of rescue workers and families waiting silently at the pithead.

To the south of the Lakes in Lancaster there was the amateur Sam Thompson and at Sunderland Point the

One hundred and thirty-six miners lost their lives in the Wellington Pit disaster. Bellman was on hand to capture all the drama. In the photograph above anxious wives await news at the pithead.

The rescue team prepare to descend but it was all to no avail. There were no survivors.

Lord Lonsdale, owner of the Wellington Pit, arrives at the pithead to inspect the rescue operation.

much ignored John Walker. Unusually for the time, there were two women photographers, the Slingsby sisters, at Grange-Over-Sands while in Barrow Edward Sankey recorded the many launches in the local shipyard though much of his work overlaps into the Edwardian era.

There were also many celebrated figures in the Lakes who at some time pressed the shutter or dabbled in the new art. It was fashionable for men of learning to engage in pursuits such as photography, astronomy, geology or natural philosophy. All those hobbies required some knowledge of science and attracted well-read, learned gentlemen to their cause. The artist John Ruskin was said to have been enchanted by the daguerreo-types he saw in Venice in 1841 and experimented with his own camera though in later life he dismissed the new art as conflicting with his anti-materialism. His devoted friend William Turner took a similar stance though for different reasons.

John Ruskin experimented with photography himself though he later dismissed the new art as conflicting with his own anti-materialism. This picture of Ruskin in reflective mood was taken by George Abraham during the 1890s.

'This is the end of art,' he lamented, 'I am glad I have had my day.' Fortunately he was wrong.

Beatrix Potter's father, Rupert, was also a photographer of some note taking more than a thousand glass plate negatives of the Lake District though he is better remembered for his portraits of his daughter and other eminent Victorians, especially his friend Sir John Millais. The artist was said to have relied heavily on Potter's photographs for his own portrait paintings and would usually have a Potter photograph propped up alongside his canvas as he painted. Sadly, most of Potter's negatives, especially those of the Lake District, have now found their way into American collections though a few still remain in this country at the Victoria and Albert Museum. But perhaps the most notable of all Lakeland photographers was Charles Lutwidge Dodgson, better known as Lewis Carroll, who took many portraits of young girls. Carroll visited friends in the Lakes regularly, taking the occasional landscape or street scene but concentrating mainly on his portraits until 1880 when he suddenly abandoned photography for reasons never fully explained.

The object of this book then is to give credit to the many

Rupert Potter's photograph of Wray Castle with Beatrix and Bertram Potter, August 1882.
(Courtesy of the Trustees of the Victoria and Albert Museum. Reproduced by permission of Frederick Warne & Co.)

photographers who hiked the fells and footpaths of the Lakes in search of a better photograph and who, thereby, helped add to the popularity of the area. Many of the photographs reproduced here have been similarly printed in other books, most of which have concentrated on recreating a Victorian image of the Lakes. While those authors gave full credit to the photographers where they could be identified, it is now time to give the photographer pride of place. The subject may be important but equally significant is the finger on the shutter. Not all the photographs in this book belong strictly to the Victorian age; some overlap into the Edwardian era but I have felt that the photographer nevertheless began life as part of that Victorian era. I trust the reader will excuse this slight

Charles Lutwidge Dodgson was better known as Lewis Carroll. Although he was not strictly speaking a Lakeland photographer he did take many photographs during his visits to the Lakes. Children, and especially young girls, featured in many of them. Both of these, previously unpublished, were taken in 1897.

eccentricity. It may also be felt that a book on Victorian Lakeland photographers should have included more landscapes. I have avoided landscapes simply because the view will have changed so little over the years and could just as easily have been taken yesterday rather than a century ago. For that reason I have tried to choose a wider selection of photographs that give some inkling of Victorian life in the Lakes.

During the course of writing this book I was approached by a number of people who remembered an Abrahams' glass plate negative or some Henry Mayson prints stored in a loft. Perhaps this book will jog a few more memories for almost certainly in an attic or two, somewhere in the Lakes, a mound of dusty old glass plate negatives is awaiting discovery and recognition. Perhaps also some day, all the glass plate negatives and prints taken by the Lakeland photographers will be gathered in a single collection under one roof where the historian, student or keen amateur can browse and view them at will.

These then are the photographers who helped popularise the Lake District and turned it from the remote and depressing outpost which the artists had painted so long ago to the popular centre it has become. Where once only a handful ventured, today millions flock. For so many years these photographers have been ignored. Hopefully, the time has now come to redress the balance and give credit where it is due.

As an Oxford don Dodgson befriended many well known figures in the world of the arts. This is the young conductor Henry Wood taken in the Lake District. He was later to become known as the founder of the Promenade Concerts.

The Abrahams

Of all the Lakeland photographers none are better known than the Abraham Brothers whose mountaineering pictures not only captured the drama of rock climbing but pioneered the use of photography on the crags. Yet the family's photographic adventures began somewhat more soberly and some distance from the Lake District.

George Perry Ashley Abraham was born in Devizes in 1844. He began work as a photographer in London with Elliot & Fry of Baker Street but later moved to Keswick to take up an apprenticeship with Alfred Pettitt at his newly established Art Gallery on Ambleside Road. Pettitt however could never quite decide whether he wanted to paint or take photographs and in 1866 after four years at Pettitt's Gallery, Abraham left to start up his own business, concentrating on studio portraits but leaving himself enough time to pursue his principal passion — landscape photography. George Abraham was a highly competent photographer who would, in time, become a Fellow of the Royal Photographic Society, and his legacy of glass plates form a fine catalogue of Victorian life. Yet it would be his sons, George Dixon Abraham and Ashley Perry Abraham who would really set the photographic world talking.

George junior was born in 1872 and his younger brother four years later. After a brief education in Keswick George was sent to Manchester Grammar School while his brother attended Blackman's Keswick School. But despite their scholarly education it was only natural that they should eventually join what had become a booming little business on Lake Road. The pioneering photographers of Keswick, Alfred Pettitt and William Ferguson were now dead leaving the market wide open to the Abrahams and the town's other photographer, Henry Mayson.

With the arrival of the railway in 1864 tourists began to flock to Keswick and by the late nineteenth century the Cumberland market town had become a thriving centre of the northern Lakes. Tourism of course meant picture postcards and the two Abraham brothers had seen just how popular they were when they holidayed at Zermatt

in Switzerland in 1898. There they had purchased cards to send to their family and friends back home in Keswick. Picture postcards were now beginning to appear in Britain and George and Ashley were among the first to realise their appeal. Tourists would want to send greetings to friends, partly as a boast of their travels, partly to convey their safe arrival. The Royal Mail was now a flourishing enterprise with cheap rates and delivery guaranteed within days of posting. All the prerequisites were set for the business to blossom. The Abrahams built a factory in the Victoria Buildings just across the street from their Lake Road hut and before long they had transferred their business over the road and a thriving industry was under way churning out postcards by the thousand displaying a hundred scenes around Derwentwater, Skiddaw and Helvellyn. And just a few doors down the road from them was Henry Mayson's photographic studio so that Lake Road soon became the obvious stop for anyone interested in photography.

Like Henry Mayson and Joseph Flintoft, George Abraham also built a relief model of the Lakes for display in the shop and it soon brought customers flocking to their premises. Lantern slide shows were another favourite with the tourists and were the ideal entertainment for rainy days. With an audience of 250 seated above their shop the Abrahams ran a racy little show, called 'A Tour of the English Lakeland, Summer and Winter, Day and Night' accompanied by a Rock and Steel Band. Not a Rock Band as we might know it today but a xylophone constructed from slates with bells made from stones. Father George would lead the way with the singing while his sons tunefully banged away on the xylophone. It was clearly popular and ran for a number of years before the family found themselves too committed to other pursuits to find time to continue with the show.

From an early age the two sons had joined their father in scrambles up the mountainside helping to carry his heavy camera and equipment in search of some new rocky promontory. They would trek the fells for miles and once the easy rambles had been conquered they turned their thoughts to the stony outcrops of the Lakes. Even before they were out of short trousers they were borrowing bits of clothes line from their mother to test on the local crags. It soon became a passion. By the time George was nineteen they had already claimed a new route to their credit at Sanbed Gill in St John's Vale and were regularly joining the growing band of experienced climbers who were venturing into the Lakes. Pillar Rock with its impressive crags and gullies was the favourite climb of the day, attracting mountaineers from all corners of the land. On most weekends George and Ashley would be found somewhere on its buttresses and precipices with a length of borrowed climbing rope. It was not long before they were also taking photographs of their mountaineering exploits and as their climbing skills improved, so too did their photographic experiments. Here was an opportunity to add even more spectacular landscapes to their portfolio as well as dramatic shots of climbers clinging to the crags. And how popular they proved. Their shop window soon became a shrine of mountaineering photographs.

One morning early in 1896 the pioneering rock climber O. G. Jones paused outside their shop. He liked the photographs he saw and had an idea. He walked into their shop and inquired if they might be interested in taking some photographs for a book he was writing. They were and a year later O. G. Jones' classic *Rock Climbing in the English Lake District* was published with more than thirty of their photographs. The book sold out immediately and soon went into a second edition, establishing their name and work among the climbing fraternity.

Photographers had never ventured onto the crags before. It was dangerous enough as it was without having to carry so much equipment and the tricky process of exposing glass plates only added to the difficulties. Their partnership with O. G. Jones was to be a rewarding venture although it would be short lived. Three years later Jones plunged to his death on the icy slopes of Dent Blanche in the Swiss Alps robbing climbing of one of its earliest exponents and enthusiasts. With Jones the two brothers broke fresh ground, setting up many exciting new climbs such as Walker's Gully on Pillar where Jones had to remove his boots in the snow and ice to reach the summit. Under his tutelage they improved their climbing technique beyond all recognition. They were deeply shocked by his death and would mourn his loss for the rest of their climbing days but it never deterred them from the crags.

Over the next forty years the Abrahams with their boundless energy would write a dozen books including *Rock Climbing in North Wales*, where they made extensive use of Jones' notes. *British Mountain Climbs*, *Swiss Mountain Climbs*, *On Alpine Heights and British Crags* and *The Complete Mountaineer* followed over the next few years. Each book was beautifully illustrated with their own photographs and usually written by George with Ashley taking the pictures.

To take these pictures the brothers would be forced to rope more than 20 pounds of equipment to their backs as they risked life and limb on the treacherous rockface. The pictures were shot on an Underwood whole plate camera using a plate with a particularly low emulsion. This meant that lengthy exposures were necessary and often led to the climber having to cling motionless to the rockface for as long as a minute while the shot was set up and a four second exposure took place. It was poor George, the lead climber who usually performed this function desperately gripping the rock by his fingertips while Ashley methodically prepared his camera.

The brothers had three lenses — a Taylor Hobson 12″ Cooke lens (f.6.8 to f.45) which was generally used for landscape shots, a similar German Goertz lens, and a Ross wide angle 6″ lens (f.16 to f.64). There were added difficulties in that none of these lenses had time exposures so that the cameraman simply had to physically remove the lens cap and replace it for the period of exposure. On top of that there were also no meters for measuring the light so that it was a case of experience, guesswork and a little luck. Usually they would experiment with a number of plates changing the exposure and even the lens to ensure that at least one shot would turn out perfectly. But the results were superb, thanks mainly to the slow emulsion which allowed for enlargements without any loss of quality and exquisitely detailed the texture of the rocks.

The brothers recorded a generation of Victorian mountaineers, climbing in hobnail boots and tweeds or in the case of women, long crinoline dresses and shawls, striking out on new unconquered routes to the summits. The Abrahams had captured forever the early years of rock climbing in Britain. It was an enchanting record though during their time they were often criticised for tampering with their plates. The line of the rockface against the sky would sometimes be sharpened to make it look more dramatic or the sky itself lightened to make silhouetted climbers stand out. It was all part of the effect but it hardly mattered, except perhaps with a few purists, and was common practice among most landscape photographers.

But the Keswick Brothers, as they soon became known, were not content simply with images of the Lakes on calm summery days. Competition in the picture postcard industry was hotting up and demanded even more spectacular scenes. So, to meet the challenge they set off for the crays in winter to capture the full glory of ice-capped mountains and snowy gullies. There it was especially dangerous, holding one's balance on the slippery ice or dug into the snow while frost-bitten fingers tried to work delicately at mixing chemicals or pressing the shutter. And once the Lakes in winter had been fully exhausted they ventured ever further afield to Skye, Ireland and then the Alps where some of their most spectacular photographs were taken.

Although George was always rated the better climber it was Ashley who became the first President of the Fell and Rock Climbing Club. He was also a fine chess player and was county champion in 1932 and later became chairman of the Keswick Urban District Council. The brothers never ceased to love climbing and only old age brought an end to their adventures though even then it was common to see them striding sprightly across the fells. In 1951 Ashley died. His brother survived him by a further fourteen years, becoming a Fellow of the Royal Photographic Society and although the family business was continued by Ashley's son Geoffrey it was eventually closed down when he retired in 1967. The business had survived 101 years and had produced some of the most memorable of all Lake District photographs.

The foyer of the Wastwater Hotel, Easter 1895, by then a natural meeting place for the growing climbing fraternity.

Mrs Sophie Bryant, a pioneering Victorian climber taken in the Abrahams' Keswick studio. A renowned Snowdonian climber she was one of the first women to attempt the peaks of the Lakes.

George Abraham near the top of Central Gully route, Gable Crag.

An ageing John Ruskin with Baxter his valet, taken during the late 1890s by George Abraham.

The great social philosopher rowing on Coniston.

Striding Edge, Helvellyn, looking east.

The Abrahams pioneered mountain photography, risking their lives as they carried their cumbersome equipment up the crags. This is the top of Pillar.

Napes Needles. First climbed in 1886 it marked the breakthrough for rock climbing in the Lakes.

As the race for more dramatic pictures quickened the Abrahams turned their attention to winter climbing, venturing not only on to snow clad peaks in the Lakes but in Wales, Scotland and the Alps as well.

Eagles Nest Ridge on Great Gable. First climbed in 1892, for many years it was the most difficult climb in the Lake District.

George Abraham brings his second up to the Sentry Box on Kern Knotts Crag.

The Abrahams produced a series of instructional photographs for climbers. This one was entitled 'The leader safeguards himself on a steep face'.

The Abbey Buttress on Gable.

William Baldry

William Baldry was a Lake District man by adoption rather than by birth. He was born in Norfolk in 1828, long before Louis Daguerre had experimented with his early exposures or Henry Ford's first cars had taken to the highways. As a young man he went off to London to run a small school for Jewish children in the East End, the main purpose of which seems to have been to baptise and convert the children to the Christian faith. It was here that Baldry met and, in 1854, married Louise Button, a maid to a lady-in-waiting at Windsor Castle. They were wed at St Mark's Church, Whitechapel and later that year the new Mrs Baldry spotted an advertisement in a newspaper seeking a master for the school just opened in Grasmere. She persuaded her husband to apply and in early 1855 Mr and Mrs Baldry set off to begin a new life in the Lake District.

Wordsworth had been dead just five years when the Baldrys arrived in the small Lakeland village where there was little of note except a few inns, a couple of shops and its famous church with the grave of the great poet. The population was no more than a few hundred and in truth the village hardly warranted a school of its own. Initially the Baldrys worked together, he teaching arithmetic and English, she instructing the girls on sewing. It might have seemed a satisfactory arrangement but a year later Baldry quit his job at the school to set up a small stationery business in the village.

Photography had not yet entered his life and precisely when it did will probably always remain a mystery but it appears that he was first introduced to the new art by a relation of his wife, possibly his brother-in-law, Edward Button, who succeeded him as schoolmaster at Grasmere. Whenever it was, Baldry quickly became an enthusiast and it was not long before his shop displayed all the baggage and paraphernalia of early photography. Glass plates would hang in the sun or rest against walls while noisy children poked their noses at the shop window awe-struck at his prints and visiting pilgrims to the nearby grave of William and Mary Wordsworth would cast more than a few curious glances at his tripod and cameras.

Baldry was now a permanent fixture in Grasmere and would have known the local artists Alfred and George Pettitt. Very likely he was instrumental in introducing Alfred Pettitt to this new art form and must have watched with some trepidation as the Pettitts began to display their own photographs in their Art Gallery. But Grasmere was clearly too small for both Baldry and Pettitt to ply the same trade and in 1858 Alfred and George packed their bags and set off for Keswick, a dozen miles up the road where photography had yet to make any impact. It left Baldry with a monopoly in the small Wordsworthian village.

By the 1870s Baldry had become a prominent figure in the tiny community. In time he would become assistant overseer, parish clerk and sexton, surveyor and inspector of nuisances and when the Grasmere Urban Council was formed he became a member of that authority. He performed a considerable amount of charitable work, helping the Volunteer Movement and was the last survivor of the original members of the Lake District Association. As if all this was not enough Baldry was to stamp his mark in a totally unexpected arena. He was to become a founder of the now famous Grasmere Sports.

It was Baldry who had introduced cricket to Grasmere in 1856 and had been honoured for his efforts by the Prince of Wales (later Edward VII), when he visited Grasmere in 1857. Baldry lent the young teenage prince a cricket bat and later received a personal letter of thanks from Buckingham Palace along with a complete cricket set for the use of the children of the village. Organised sport had barely filtered into the Lakes before the turn of the century. The Football League would not be formed until 1888 and there is little evidence that the game appeared in the Lakes much before 1892 although rugby was being played by 1871. The only sports were those traditional to the countryside — fox-hunting, fishing, shooting and horse racing and some home-spun Lakeland sports such as Cumberland Wrestling. Baldry and others, including the Earl of Lonsdale, hit upon the idea of an organised sporting gala that would embrace some of these Lakeland sports. A race, to the summit of nearby

Silverhow had been held in 1852 and in 1868 it was resurrected as the focal attraction of the new Games with a prize of £3 to the winner. It was known as the Guides' Race but a number of other sports were also included in the one-day programme such as Cumberland wrestling, a one mile race, a hound trail, a boat race, pole leaping and the high leap. One hundred and twenty-five years later the event, now known as the Grasmere Sports, is still going strong.

It was hardly surprising that Baldry should pick up his equipment from the back of the shop and stroll across to Hudson's Field, next door to the Red Lion Hotel where the Prince of Wales had stayed, to become the official photographer. Sports photography was still in its infancy. Even a national game like football had rarely been photographed before 1880 and then it was usually posed portraits or team pictures. There was little on-the-spot recording of events. It was complicated. Not only did cumbersome equipment have to be carted around and painstakingly set up close to the activity but action shots with their speed presented a special problem for photographers. The Victorian photographer's lens could not cope and wherever there was movement there was a blur on the developed print. Yet Baldry overcame all these difficulties. By positioning himself a little distance from his subject he was able to take high speed all-action photographs of Cumberland wrestling, pole leaping and long jumping. Even by today's quality they are fine pictures; by the standards of the 1870s and 80s they were unique, presenting not only a wonderful history of the early days of the Grasmere Sports but a fascinating insight into Lakeland life. All the old glass plates have now sadly been lost but they were reprinted in 1911 in a rare volume entitled *Some Records of the Annual Grasmere Sports* by Hugh Machell and Canon Rawnsley.

And when the Games were over there was still work to be done. The champions would each want their photograph taken and in his studio at the back of the shop Baldry built a suitable mock-up background in front of which the winning contestants could pose. The champion fell racer of the 1880s, John Grizedale, was photographed ready to leap a country fence while champion wrestler George Steadman stood proudly alongside his growing collection of medals, trophies and belts. The winning hounds were also brought in and photographed with their proud owners in front of the same country fences.

It has to be admitted however that there is evidence that Baldry retouched some of his action pictures in order to make them sharper but that should not detract from the overall quality which remains as high as was technically possible at the time. His great rival at the Games was the Ambleside photographer Lovell Mason who captured some equally fine action shots, especially of the Cumberland wrestling and its great champion, George Steadman. But Mason's pictures lack the overall perspective of Baldry's. They are confined mainly to wrestling and pole leaping and although they are a valuable collection they do not represent as broad a record of the games.

Had Baldry's pictures of the Grasmere Sports been his only contribution to photography then he would still remain an important figure, yet he made one other major contribution — he became the official photographer of the Thirlmere Dam project. The back-breaking work of constructing a dam and flooding the Thirlmere valley to provide water for the City of Manchester began in 1890. It was a massive engineering project, bigger than anything ever seen in the Lake District, and was a mere half dozen miles up the road from Grasmere over Dunmail Raise. The flooding of the valley caused uproar among Lakeland folk. Canon Rawnsley who was later to become the founder of the National Trust was bitterly opposed to the project, angered at the disappearance of many small hamlets, including his favourite at Wythburn where only the small church remained. The Bishop of Carlisle also wrote a furious letter of complaint to *The Times* that began an earnest debate in the letters and editorial columns of the national press. Baldry was also opposed to the £5 million scheme yet it offered him the unique opportunity to capture the changing environment of the Lakes. Not only did he chronicle a scene that no longer exists as he photographed the villages in the valley that are today under water but he recorded the back-breaking work of a major engineering feat.

Baldry was a regular visitor to the site, so regular that the project engineer, a German, became a close friend. His welcoming hand at Thirlmere was soon reciprocated by the Baldry household where he would become a regular visitor. And when Baldry's son Edward was born he was given the second name Hermann in appreciation of his father's friendship with the German engineer. Baldry photographed work at Thirlmere from the beginning and was there at the end as the civic dignitaries of Manchester descended on Grasmere for the opening ceremony in February 1894.

Baldry was not a man to go scaling the heights of the local crags. He was far too respectable for that kind of rash adventure. He might occasionally take off up the fells with his camera but most of his work was done in and around Grasmere. He was a well-built, slightly stout man sporting a magnificent full beard, a teetotaller, a regular church goer, and a devoted husband and father. He had four sons and four daughters, only one of whom, Edward Hermann, followed him into the photography business.

The Baldry shop continued to thrive and later became a large general stores. Today it is a small coffee shop, still adopting his name and with one or two of his pictures of the Games adorning its walls. Baldry died in August 1918 at the age of ninety, surviving his wife by four years, leaving behind a rich legacy of life in and around the tiny hamlet of Grasmere.

As a founding member of the Grasmere Sports it was hardly surprising that William Baldry should also become its official photographer. The Games began in 1868 and for the next thirty years Baldry recorded its many activities. This is the central arena around 1870.

Cumberland wrestling was also a top attraction at the sports and nobody was more popular than its greatest exponent George Steadman, seen here fighting George Lowden for the champion's belt. Steadman was champion for more than thirty years, finally retiring in 1900.

John Grizedale, perhaps the most famous of all fell racers, trained on beef, eggs, chicken, port and brandy. As the official photographer Baldry would invite the winners to his studio in Grasmere where their photograph would be taken in front of some makeshift scenery.

Cumberland Wrestling at the 1873 Sports. The Games soon attracted the gentry of the day and the August event quickly became a regular part of the social calendar.

The centre of attraction at the Games was, and still is, the Guides Race, a short sprint to the top of nearby Silverhow and back. As their name suggests the guides were professionals who guided the tourists across the fells. There was also a competition for the best dressed guide.

Postman Pat delivering the Royal Mail to the Swan Inn at Grasmere.

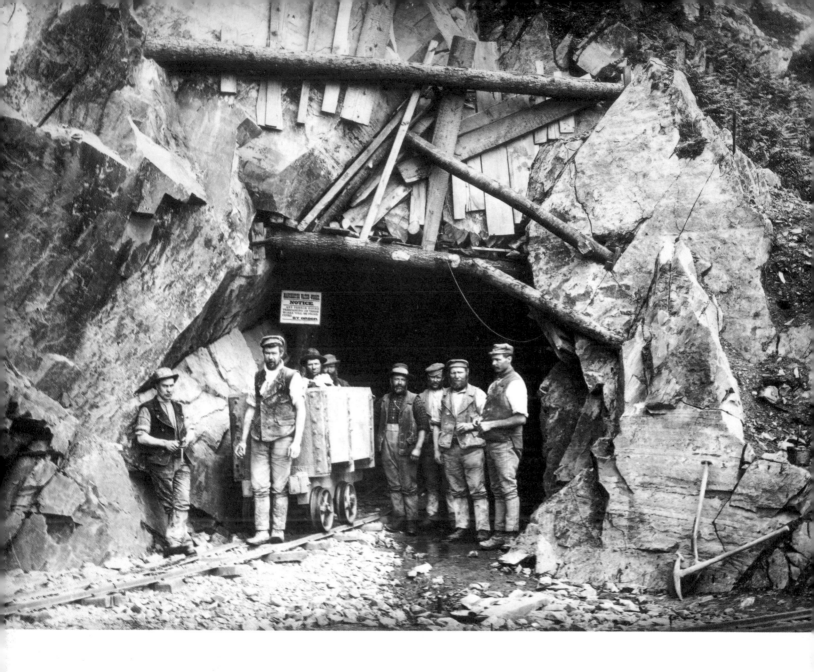

Baldry's other claim to fame was to record the construction of the Thirlmere Reservoir and Dam. Work began in 1890 and went on for the next four years. It was a massive engineering project, the likes of which the lakes had never seen.

THIRLMERE. No. 2 DAM OCTOBER

The work involved flooding the valley with the result that many small hamlets tragically disappeared under water. This is the Cherry Tree Inn, once a regular watering hole of William Wordsworth. It has long since disappeared to help quench the thirst of Mancunians, almost a hundred miles away.

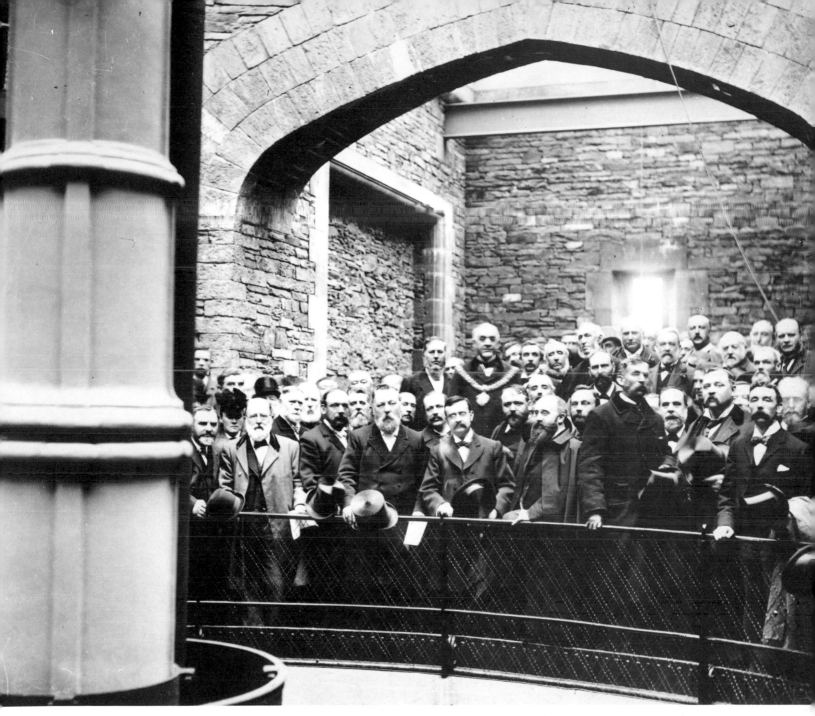

Manchester's nobility, including the Lord Mayor and councillors arrive at the Pump House for the opening ceremony, February 1894.

Herbert Bell

Herbert Bell was born in Ambleside in 1856, the son of a chemist and mineral water manufacturer whose shop in Lake Road still stands today. Photography was barely twenty years old and had yet to reach the small Lakeland village, population less than 2,000, where the main economic activities still centred around the agricultural community. Tourism had yet to arrive although the coming of steam further down the valley at Windermere was beginning to gradually change the commercial life of the area. Even in 1873 *Kelly's Trade Directory* listed only two photographers in Ambleside, Moses Bowness and Thomas Garside. It would be a few more years before the town began to rival Windermere for the tourist's attention.

Bell's early schooling was at Eller How in Ambleside where he studied under the formidable Mrs Clough, later to become the first principal of Newnham College, Cambridge. He later transferred to the Stramonsgate school at Kendal and on completion of his studies moved into his father's shop to begin an apprenticeship that would eventually take him from stirring chemicals for medicines to mixing chemicals for developing photographs. It was not unusual in those days for chemist shops to also dabble in photography as the new art required a wide range of chemicals, all of which would be available from the chemist's.

The mixing of chemicals for the photographer's trade would be carried out in the backroom of the shop and involved the use of chemicals such as bromide, iodide salts and collodion. The procedure fascinated Herbert and it was not long before his interest quickly shifted from the development of photographs to actually taking them. It was impossible to understand photography without a basic understanding of science so that a chemist was ideally placed to pursue the interest. Science was becoming increasingly popular and it was fashionable among learned men to take up a science pursuit such as geology, astronomy or phrenology. Photography fitted into this definition and between 1860 and 1900 attracted many intellectual men (and a few women) to its cause including, of course, Herbert Bell.

But his father's shop was still primarily concerned with medicines and life for the young Bell selling vapour inhalers, foot warmers and chest protectors seemed a far cry from the romantic world of the photographer. By the 1890s, possibly earlier, he had decided where his future lay. He would set up his own business concentrating on photography, leaving his father to look after the chemist shop and its sickly customers. Finding premises was not too difficult and before long he had opened up a studio in Market Square and by 1894 was listed in *Kelly's Trade Directory* as photographer. It was the beginning of a long romance that would establish Bell as one of the finest Lakeland photographers of the era. Within the next two years he would have taken some of his finest pictures.

When the Lakes iced over during the arctic winter of 1894/1895 Bell was there, no doubt huddled in layers of boots and coats, to capture the historic moment. Windermere was frozen solid from end to end with 18 inches of ice for seven weeks during February and March 1895 attracting hordes of day trippers from Manchester and Lancashire as they took full advantage of the special cheap rail excursions offered for the occasion. Thousands pulled on their skates or took to toboggans. At one point in early February temperatures plummeted to minus seventeen as blizzards raged across the Lakes. There was snow everywhere with drifts of six or seven feet even in the valleys and icicles dangling more than ten feet. Any ground above 100 feet was unpassable.

For most businessmen the snow was a curse. Nobody went shopping, roads were blocked, farmers in the remote valleys were trapped and animals died by the score on the lonely freezing fells. But for Herbert Bell it provided a unique opportunity. When would the Lakes ever appear so tranquil and when would Windermere again be as frozen? Not only that but there was an unexpected bonanza to be made from the sudden influx of tourists at what was normally a quiet time of the year. As they streamed off the trains and made their way down to the Lake Bell was there to meet them, his tripod carefully erected on the slippery ice. It could not have been an easy task for him. Chemicals had to be mixed and carefully measured with frozen fingers and trying to maintain his balance while hidden behind his dark tent must have been a tricky manoeuvre. No doubt he lost a few glass plates as they slipped from his fingers. Also there was the technical challenge of producing a sharp negative while battling against so much light. Yet Bell was equal to the task.

Herbert Bell of course was not alone in realising the potential of the occasion. William Brunskill, the Bowness photographer was also quick off the mark as the two rivalled one another for custom among the skating hordes. Bell was not going to settle for the quieter northern end of the Lake near his Ambleside studio but ventured instead into Brunskill's territory near Bowness pier where the travellers would arrive by coach or on foot from Windermere station. Brunskill was said to be none too pleased at Bell infringing on his patch but the two maintained a respectful distance, especially when they were also joined on the ice by other photographers. But there was clearly more than enough custom for all of them as the crowds continued arriving each weekend until the ice dramatically began to crack under the March thaw.

Bell's photographs of fun and games on the Lake helped establish his name in the growing world of photography and later that year, in August 1895, he would have a second scoop when Kaiser Wilhelm of Germany visited Lakeland. After a brief stay at Cowes and lunch at Osborne House, Isle of Wight, with Queen Victoria the Kaiser journeyed north on the Royal train to Whitehaven where he stayed at Lowther Castle as a guest of his friend Lord Lonsdale. Bell was again on hand to record this special event in Lakeland life. The Kaiser's visit although inevitably disrupted by the rain involved a sail on Windermere, lunch at the Old England Hotel in Bowness and the journey to Ambleside, Grasmere and Keswick where he boarded a train for Penrith and points further north. Lakeland turned out in force welcoming him with bunting and loud generous cheers. Twenty years later the same cheering crowds would be marching to do battle with the Kaiser and his army.

Perhaps one of Bell's greatest achievements was to compile a photographic record of all the farms and memorial halls of Cumberland and Westmorland. The collection is of special interest being the only record of so many buildings now in ruins or long since disappeared. His sensitively produced photographs, many of which were taken on a Meacher box camera made in Southampton, are an architectural historian's delight though they may not be of quite so much interest to others. He also illustrated a number of books and was commissioned by George Allen and Unwin to prepare various plates for their weighty tomes on John Ruskin.

But Bell's qualities were not confined to crumbling buildings and frolics on the ice. He had a keen eye and wandered around his home town of Ambleside, photographing washerwomen, sheep shearers and huntsmen. Here was a social view of Ambleside that contrasted starkly with the romantic image of this rural Lakeland town. He even took his camera further afield to Hartsop where he photographed miners and to Thirlmere where he captured the cruel work of turning a valley into a reservoir for the city of Manchester.

Bell soon became a pillar of Lakeland society. The Ruskin Society met in his studio and on many a wintery evening Canon Rawnsley, Albert Fleming and Mary Armitt might be found huddled around his fireplace discussing the merits of the master himself, John Ruskin. From here opposition to a proposal to extend the railway from Windermere to Ambleside was mounted with Rawnsley and Bell bitterly opposing any such scheme while Mary Armitt argued forcibly in favour. From its inception Bell was active in the Armitt library at Ambleside and was honorary librarian between 1912 and 1946 as well as a member of the Dove Cottage local committee and the National Trust. He also travelled widely taking his camera wherever he journeyed returning with some fine negatives of Germany, Austria, Scotland and Ireland.

A gentle and courteous man with fine features, far seeing blue eyes and a sturdy constitution, he had first taken to the fells as a ten year old boy. He knew them well, had scaled most mountains, crossed most valleys and lovingly portrayed most landscapes. His final stroll across the heathland would be on his eightieth birthday. Ten years later on November 1st 1946 he died.

The ruined cloisters of Furness Abbey. Herbert Bell spent much of his time roaming the countryside photographing the old farms and memorial halls of Cumberland and Westmorland. Today they form a unique record of architectural history.

'A foot above men's common measure tall . . . Stiff in his form, and upright, lank and lean.' (Wordsworth)
George Smith, the Skiddaw Hermit who died in 1875. Smith turns up in the portfolios of many of the Lakeland photographers.

The ferry boat crossing Lake Windermere with horse-drawn carriages around 1880.

Victorian Ambleside, busy even before the tourist invasion.

Within a few years Ambleside had become a stop on the tourist trail.

A washerwoman in Ambleside.

Bell and friends try their hand at golf on a fairway that looks a little rougher than today's versions.

This is probably a self portrait of Bell on one of his camping and photographic expeditions.

Gales could bring havoc to the Lakes and Bell would walk miles to record anything out of the ordinary.

Fly fishing in the days when salmon and trout abounded in the streams and rivers of the Lakes.

A lunch break for Victorian ramblers.

The great freeze of 1895. On one February Saturday more than 7,000 pulled on their ice skates and ventured onto Windermere. For six weeks most of Lakeland was frozen as temperatures dipped to minus fifteen.

Charcoal Burners pause for lunch. 'Slowly the cooled mound is turned back. The tired burners smile. The prize, the charcoal, glistens satin-black, and rings clear as a bell,' wrote Irvine Hunt.

One of the most celebrated of all Lakeland photographs. Robinson Mawson Pattison of Thorn House shearing a Herdwick, taken around 1885.

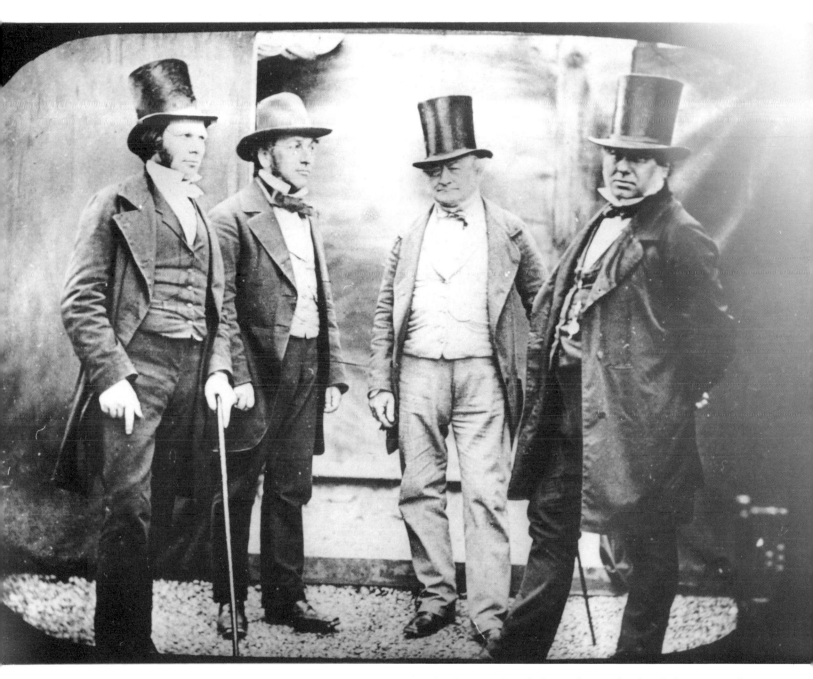

These four gentlemen were said to be good friends of William Wordsworth. They are, from left to right: Dr Shepherd, the Reverend Tatham, Mr Smith and Dr Fell.

The construction of Thirlmere reservoir was a major engineering feat. Equipment, including pipes, had to be hauled across the mountains and through the villages of the Lake District by horse and cart.

The Herberts

It is surprising how an interest in photography has been passed from generation to generation, particularly among the Lakeland photographers where whole families have often dabbled successfully. George Abraham in Keswick passed on his skill to his sons George junior and Ashley; William Baldry's son Edward Hermann was an equally accomplished photographer; and at Bowness the Herberts straddled three generations.

The founder of Bowness' mini-photographic-dynasty, Robert Herbert began life about as far removed from photography as imaginable. Born in Durham in 1823 his early career had included taxidermy and bloodletting. He had even tried his hand at a spot of poaching and hairdressing before he eventually turned to photography. He was almost certainly one of the first in the north east to tinker in the new art and he took to it like a fish to water. Yet it was to be his son, Henry, who would cross the Pennines and pursue the trade with even more distinction in the Lake District.

Henry Herbert was born in 1858 and came to Bowness during the 1880s to serve an apprenticeship with William Brunskill, the accomplished Bowness and Windermere cameraman. It was to be the beginning of a long and fruitful relationship with the Lakes. Working alongside Brunskill, Henry learnt not only the rudiments of his art though he had already arrived with a fundamental knowledge, but now discovered the more subtle approaches which would distinguish the professional from the good amateur. Brunskill was an especially skilled craftsman with a fine understanding of light and shade and his influence on Herbert can easily be spotted. Brunskill taught his pupil well.

Henry however was an innovator and not content to sit at the feet of Brunskill for very long. By 1894 he had his own shop at Bank Terrace in Bowness and was soon beginning to rival his master for trade. Brunskill may have been a superb landscape artist but when it came to business he was no match for Henry Herbert who was always on the lookout for new opportunities or some technically superior piece of equipment. When Windermere froze over during the wretched winter of 1895 Henry Herbert was first on the ice with his camera taking portraits of the skaters at a shilling a time. It was easy money and highly popular among the thousands of tourists flocking towards Bowness to see the spectacular sight of Windermere frozen solid. Not surprisingly he was soon joined by Herbert Bell who skated down from Ambleside to steal some of the action. Brunskill also joined them on the ice when he saw the brisk trade Herbert was drawing. There was more than enough work for the three of them but it had been Henry Herbert who had shown the commercial instinct.

Business thrived and Henry was always on the scene no matter what the occasion recording the event so that it could later be sold as a postcard. The tourist industry was suddenly beginning to expand as workers, particularly from Lancashire, took advantage of cheap rail excursions. Before long the demand for postcards was outstripping supply as the visitors purchased the cards to send greetings to their friends back home. Yet even here Henry Herbert was not one to be satisfied at producing a variety of scenes on simple postcards. He was one of the first locals to follow a national trend by designing postcards with a greetings slogan in a lucky horseshoe. It was all part of the competition and challenge of producing a better quality postcard for the discerning market.

Henry Herbert could not scale the crags like the Abraham brothers in Keswick, nor capture a memorable moment like Walmsley but he was inventive and original and he passed his entrepreneurial talent on to his two sons, Louis born in 1882, and Frank in 1890. Before they were ten years old the two boys were being dragged up nearby Orrest Head and Miller Brow on photographic expeditions. Soon they were racing ahead of their father helping him carry the heavy equipment or steadying him as he retreated behind his black tent to begin the lengthy process of exposing his wet plate picture. It was not long before they too had cameras and were seriously learning the new art. By the turn of the century Louis was already behind the counter at his father's shop assimilating the business and was to be joined a few years later by Frank.

The lads were keen, happy to go places their ageing father considered beyond him. They would stride across fells he was growing too weary to trek or dash about the countryside on errands and photographic missions. It was all part of their training but the day would soon arrive when they would teach their father a trick or two. In 1912 young Frank persuaded his father to cough up a few pounds for a daring aeroplane flight across Bowness. It was only three years since Louis Bleriot had made his dashing flight across the Channel and only six months since Stanley Adams had piloted the first plane over the Lakes. Father Herbert was not too keen, reckoning it far too dangerous but under pressure from both sons he eventually relented. It was to be money well spent that would put Frank Herbert in the record books as the first man to photograph the Lake District from the air.

And so, on April 30th 1912 with Frank Herbert in the passenger seat and Stanley Adams again piloting, a small waterplane rose gently into the air from Hill of Oaks at the southern end of Windermere. It was a fragile craft to say the least. Named *Waterhen* and with no chassis, just a couple of floats, the plane was owned by Captain Edward Wakefield, a Kendal businessman. With no protection against the buffeting wind, Frank leaned out of the passenger seat and anxiously pointed his half plate camera towards Bowness pier where his father and brother watched excitedly and no doubt anxiously with a crowd of startled onlookers. As the rattling plane approached and banked they waved and Frank captured the moment for posterity. Soon he was rising high above the Lake, leaning first one way, then the other, taking dramatic aerial shots of Windermere that would soon be transformed into a thousand postcards. It was an enormous success and the whole venture owed much to Frank's daring endeavour. Before long *Waterhen* had become a permanent fixture on Windermere regularly taking the more wealthy tourists on £2 flights over the Lake.

Frank may have been the daring member of the family but Louis had the more wicked sense of humour and on one famous occasion foxed thousands of their customers by producing a sensational photograph of an animal called the Tizzie-Whizzie. Of course there was no such creature, it was a mock-up of a mouse with wings, and was secretly taken by Louis in 1906 in their studio. But the resulting photograph caused a minor sensation and while Louis could keep a straight face, hundreds of gullible customers bought copies of the photograph. The locals all laughed but the visitors were no doubt annoyed to have been taken in so easily.

It was not the first time the Herberts had doctored a picture and it would not be the last. Indeed it was almost a regular and endearing feature of their work. Sometimes a plane might suddenly appear where none had been present when the exposure was made. Or, more likely, swans might be seen gliding gracefully in the foreground when they were actually up the other end of the Lake. But it was only ever minor doctoring simply to make a postcard more commercial or pleasing to the eye. And, after all, it was a common technique among many of the Lakeland photographers. Indeed a widely read book of the time was *Taking and Faking Photographs*.

In 1915 they photographed Lord and Lady Baden-Powell when they visited Bowness and four years later they recorded the First World War victory parade through the streets of the town. There were also fairs, elections and Coronation parades as well as the arrival of the first automobiles. In June 1930 they sensationally photographed Sir Henry Seagrave on his final fatal attempt to break the world water speed record. When Henry Herbert died in 1928 his two sons carried on the business of chronicling life in and around the Lakes until they retired in 1960. At one time they were employing ten staff in their studios as they poured out postcards by the thousand. They have left a lasting legacy not only of postcards but hundreds of portraits that stretched over more than sixty years. Yet after three generations of taking photographs there was nobody remaining to continue the trade and the famous family firm of Herbert Brothers disappeared from the streets of Bowness. Louis died in 1972 and his brother Frank, four years later.

Queen Victoria's Golden Jubilee of 1887 was celebrated in fine style. At Bowness they erected a splendid arch of foliage while on Lake Windermere the Steam Yacht Britannia was suitably decked out in flags and bunting. And in the town a band appeared to celebrate the occasion giving the photographers, including Henry Herbert, a field day.

Another famous Lakeland occasion, the wretched winter of 1895 when Lake Windermere froze from end to end for six weeks with 18 inches of ice. As trainloads of skaters descended on the Lakes the enterprising photographers were quick off the mark to erect their tripods and make a few shillings from the amazed visitors.

This photograph from Fenty's album taken by Henry Herbert commemorated the visit in August 1890 of the bearded Li Hung Chang, Viceroy of China. Photographed with his entourage and guests it is a splendid scene of British pride and Oriental mystery, a copy of which was almost certainly carried back to China.

The arrival of the car in the Lakes later brought in a flood of tourists but initially it was a centre of attraction, not just for gawping schoolchildren but for the photographers as well.

A gentle boating scene from Henry Herbert, displaying his artistic eye.

A church parade around the turn of the century with fancy dress, flags and banners.

The enterprising Herberts quickly realised the photographic potential of flying and in April 1912 Frank Herbert was the first photographer to take a camera into the skies over the Lakes. For the picture postcard industry it opened up a whole new vista.

William Lawrie

Telophoto lenses are an integral part of the photographer's baggage today but at the turn of the century such lenses were unknown. All that existed was a lens with a long focal length which hardly warranted the description 'telephoto'. If you wanted a close-up, then you simply moved closer to your subject. This was fine as long as you were able to get nearer and your subject consented. But when it came to photographing animals it was almost impossible. Like sport, animal photography was in its infancy still awaiting the development of lenses that could cope with the demands of the photographer. Yet despite all the difficulties it did not deter some from attempting the impossible. William Carruthers Lawrie was one such man who with only the basic equipment stalked the craggy mountainsides or lay quietly in his hide hoping to record the bird life of the Lake District.

W. C. Lawrie was born on July 3rd 1883, the son of Thomas Adam Lawrie and Mary Johnstone Carruthers who had married a few years earlier in Workington Presbyterian Church. His father was an accountant employed at the Oldside Iron Works in Workington, a town that had been churning out iron since 1763. By the late nineteenth century Workington was still dependent on its iron and coal mining industries although it was no longer as important a port as it had been when 160 ships were employed in the exporting of coal. Yet despite the apparent comfort and status of his profession, Thomas Adam decided that accountancy was not for him. He had become interested in photography, influenced perhaps by James Bellman, an outstanding Victorian photographer who operated just a few miles down the coast at Whitehaven.

Shortly after the birth of William his father decided to open a photography business in Kingston-on-Thames though why he did not choose Workington will forever remain a mystery. Perhaps he imagined business might be better in the south. If he did, he was wrong, for the enterprise failed miserably leaving him with considerable debts. A sad and somewhat disillusioned man he emigrated to America with his family, settling first in Detroit and then in 1894 at St Joseph in Michigan. But the New World offered little improvement. Times were hard, work was scarce, the family was poor and in the end there was little alternative but to send William and his three sisters along with their mother back to England where at least he knew they would be cared for by their family.

William Carruthers Lawrie had left school in America at the age of twelve and had begun work as a printer's devil on a local newspaper. To be suddenly uprooted and returned to the solitude of Workington can hardly have been an easy experience for the young lad especially as he was immediately sent back to school. But in his spare time he did begin to work in his grandfather's chemist shop. From chemist to photographer was but a short step, especially when his own father had already introduced him to the new art. It was ironic that William should pursue the one business his father had dreamed of and failed at. That he should successfully practise it in his father's home town only added to the irony.

To gain wider experience Lawrie briefly left Workington and moved to Keswick where he found work at the chemist shop in Market Square. Here he came into contact with George Abraham and Henry Mayson, two of the Lake District's outstanding photographers, who both owned studios on Lake Road. No doubt they would have been regular customers at the chemist shop purchasing their endless supplies of chemicals and no doubt with his growing interest in photography the young Lawrie would have fallen into excited conversation with them. In Keswick he also met Annie Agnes Hodgson, the daughter of a local boatbuilder, who would eventually become his wife. But Lawrie had barely been in Keswick a few months when word reached him that his grandfather, back in Workington, could not cope alone. Old age had finally caught up with him and the chemist shop at 105 Corporation Road, Workington was his if he wanted it. He rushed home to seize the opportunity and quickly agreed a price with his grandfather. From being a chemist's assistant Lawrie suddenly had a pharmaceutical business of his own. Some time later his grandfather died and the little money that was left to him was sufficient to bring the pining Agnes the twenty or so miles from Keswick to Workington where they were married in September 1911. Before long Lawrie's chemist shop had taken on a different appearance. It was soon advertised as a 'Photographic Chemists' with increasing emphasis on the photographic side of the business. Camera equipment and chemicals soon cluttered the windows pushing the embrocations and herbal remedies aside.

Ever since he was a child Lawrie had nurtured a love of bird watching, often stalking the local fields and mountains near his Michigan home in search of eggs. It was a typical boyhood pursuit that eventually became a passion. When he returned to England he could hardly have come to a finer spot for bird watching than the Lake District. Here along the sand dunes, up craggy ridges, or close to the calm waters of the lakes could be detected a wealth of bird life — peregrines, hawks, buzzards, tawny owls, terns, rooks, carrion, heron and even the occasional eagle. It was little wonder that his hobby should have flourished when he returned. At first his interest was confined to spotting nests and collecting eggs (something which no doubt would be severely frowned on today) but as it grew more serious he decided one spring afternoon to take his camera with him.

He had built a hide close to some peregrine nests at Mellbreak near Bassenthwaite where he had been watching the young birds hatch and take their first steps into the wide world. If only he could photograph them so that others could enjoy the sight. It was worth a try and his carefully constructed hide was probably within easy shooting range. So that afternoon he set up his camera, using a small tripod which he had assembled at home the previous evening, and sat back to await the mother with a supply of food. He did not have to wait long. The young chicks were far too busy feeding and making their own noise to hear Lawrie quietly pressing the shutter and changing his plates. Within the hour he had snapped a series of photographs that would give a new lease of life to his passion and draw admiration from his friends and acquaintances.

From then on whenever Lawrie went bird watching his camera went with him. More hides were built, and revisited each year as the birds returned and fresh fledglings hatched. Lawrie took to documenting it all in detail so that the development and growth of the birds could be spotted through his photographic record. Dozens of exercise books were filled with his observations as he chronicled the life of each bird and its nesting habits. And eggs by the hundred were collected, carefully blown and then wrapped in cotton wool to preserve them. Today they all lie in the vaults of the Helena Thompson Museum in Workington, awaiting a permanent exhibition. It was unique. Who else had photographed the young peregrines and buzzards of the Lake District so closely, and all before the First World War?

Every Thursday on half day closing during the spring and summer and on a Sunday, Lawrie would load a bundle of equipment on to the back of his bike and cycle off towards Bassenthwaite or Loweswater. There he would make for each hide and spend a few hours recording the latest developments before moving off to another hide. Among his baggage would be a plate camera in a strong leather case with an extended bellow, a second camera with spare dark slides, a long focal lens, a short heavy wooden tripod, a coil of rope and a number of wooden slats which would be used for constructing new hides. As soon as he spotted a new nest under construction or one with eggs his hide would be meticulously built, then camouflaged with leaves and bracken, leaving just enough space for him to peer out with his camera. Then it would be visited twice a week until the chicks were hatched and he could begin photographing. And where it was impossible to set up a hide he even risked lowering himself down the rockface by rope. With his camera tied around his neck he would slither down the rock until he could find a ledge where he could set up his equipment.

He always used a dry plate camera which though perhaps not affording him the finest quality at least gave him more flexibility in the confines of his den where it would have been almost impossible to have used a wet plate camera. Indeed Lawrie was so fond of his dry plate camera that even in 1959, long after the introduction of 35mm cameras, he was still devoted to his old favourite that had served him so well over the years.

Aside from his ornithological photography there was much else to commend Lawrie. He took thousands of portraits of the townsfolk of Workington and also shot many street scenes in and around Workington which were sold as postcards. Yet he took surprisingly few landscapes. He did however take some fine industrial photographs, particularly during the bitter 1912 coal strike which left Workington and its many mining families scrabbling for coal and food to make ends meet. He later turned to commercial photography illustrating the building of the coke ovens at the Workington Iron and

Steel Company's plant, and the sinking of the Solway Colliery during the 1930s.

A witty and engaging man, Lawrie was slim and agile with soft features, greying hair and a moustache. For many years he was President of the Ramblers' Association and was also a skilled joiner, building much of the furniture for his home and family as well as various pieces of equipment for his photographic activities such as tripods. He died on September 30th 1960, at the age of 77.

One of Lawrie's earliest photographs taken on the dockside at Workington, then still a busy and important port.

The great national mining strike, March 1912. Desperate for fuel, miners and their families scrabble for coal near Clifton in West Cumberland. The three month long strike was called to secure a minimum wage of five shillings (25p) a shift for men and two shillings (10p) for boys.

The Furness Railway near Workington prior to the First World War, an important means of transport both for the miners and their coal.

The early aviators caused a sensation especially when their planes arrived for air displays at outposts such as Workington.

Lawrie was perhaps best known for his ornithological photographs. Taken at a time when powerful lenses were still unknown he had to rely instead on a good lair and plenty of patience.

Once Lawrie had constructed his hide, he would return at least once a week, waiting for eggs to hatch or a mother to return with her feed.

An owl waits patiently for dusk.

Peregrines on their nests below the crags at Mellbreak, near Bassenthwaite.

Another excellent close-up shot; this time of a gull on the beach.

Lawrie at his finest. Not just a bird photographer but a photographer capable of capturing the mood of the dunes and sands on Cumberland's bleak west coast.

Henry Mayson

By the 1890s Keswick with a population of almost 5,000 was a bustling little market town on the northern fringes of the Lake District. Unlike Ambleside and Grasmere it was directly connected to the rail network and was just as accessible for the visitor. The Penrith to Keswick line had opened in 1864 and by 1886 Mancunians could buy a third class return for 18 shillings (90p) while those north of the Lakes, in Glasgow, could travel down for much the same price. Coupled with cheap rail fares, and especially the cheap day excursion, came the six day week and regular holidays for many industrial workers. Tourism was about to flourish and Keswick, perfectly situated on the edge of Derwentwater, was set to capitalise on the boom. Yet as *Baddeley's* tourist guide for the time noted 'here the tourist perceives no divided duty . . . it is Keswick or nowhere'.

Picturesque though it was, Keswick, as the guidebook suggested, sat isolated among the bleak peaks of the northern hills. Once off the train, you were trapped with little in the way of alternative transport to make your escape. And on rainy days there was not, to say the least, much in the way of entertainment. Yet that hardly seemed to deter the visitors who rolled up in increasing numbers and despite the apparent lack of indoor amusement anyone visiting Keswick in the middle of the last century could at least while away a wet afternoon in the Town Hall wandering around Joseph Flintoft's model of the Lakes. Flintoft, born in the North Riding of Yorkshire, had come to the Lakes to hunt and shoot but had soon grown tired of those pursuits and had then spent seven years modelling a relief map of the Lakes on a 3-inch to the mile scale. It was a superb model that drew custom and comment for many years and would eventually help establish one of the Lakes most famous photographers. He was Henry Mayson.

Mayson was born one of eleven children in 1845 and set up in business as a photographer on Lake Road during the early 1880s. He had been quick to spot the success of Flintoft's model and decided a rival model was now called for. But whereas the agile Flintoft had hiked across every valley and summit of the Lakes to measure and draw his precise model, Mayson benefitted from the newly published ordnance survey maps. It made his task that much easier and he was able to construct a model at 6 inches to the mile, twice the size of Flintoft's. It measured 12 feet 9 inches by 9 feet 3 inches and at a shilling (5p) a time was even cheaper than the masterpiece in the Town Hall.

Here the visitor could spend a few hours examining the troughs and peaks of Cumberland and Westmorland, so delicately traced and coloured on a giant board, rather like a model railway layout. And if you could not make it during the day, then there was always the evening when gas lamps would eerily light up his large shop. It was not long before Flintoft's model had been relegated from pride of place and the tourists were instead flocking towards Lake Road and Henry Mayson's superior template. It was recommended by G. B. Airey, the Astronomer Royal and Dr Ryle, the Lord Bishop of Liverpool and went on to make Mayson a handsome profit even though a third rival, photographer George Abraham, just a few doors away in Lake Road, built yet another on a similar scale to Mayson's.

Mayson used his model of the Lakes as a springboard to set up a photography business though by the 1880s there were already rivals with Pettitt's Gallery and George Abraham's photographic studios both well established. Alfred Pettitt's Gallery had been in existence since 1858 while George Abraham had been running a shop on Lake Road since 1866. It may have seemed that there was little room for a third party, yet Mayson managed to carve out a niche for himself. But in truth, his most lucrative days were already past. Visitors eventually tired of his model and as a commercial photographer he could not challenge the Abrahams with their dramatic mountaineering photographs nor Pettitt's Gallery with its fine collection of portraits and oil paintings. Business plummeted and became so poor that Mayson was often forced to find a sideline and for a time even ran a circulating library. Yet all this is to undervalue Henry Mayson who was an outstanding photographer.

Fortunately many of his glass plate negatives have

survived the rigours of time and have been reproduced to give testimony to the quality of his work. Unlike so many of the Lakeland photographers Mayson actually enjoyed studio work. From time to time he would venture out into the wild with his tripod and camera but he was more likely to be found somewhere in his shop, and usually upstairs, processing, enlarging or framing his portraits. It is hard to choose between his rural photographs which have a quality not unlike Charles Walmsley's pictures, and his studio portraits which chronicle the townsfolk of Keswick.

Mayson was also a fisherman and had a further sideline in selling fishing licences for the Lake and the rivers above Ouse Bridge. And after their day's fishing the fishermen would invariably drop in on their way home to display proudly their catch before the camera. The bowler-hatted Mr Coulthard lifted his mammoth salmon, no doubt hooked on the Greta sometime in the late autumn when the salmon were said to be especially active. Other catches were usually much humbler. There were bridal groups as well, posing blissfully for the camera, football teams and cricket elevens manfully sporting their winning trophies, and the local volunteer fire brigade who turned up at the studio every year for their annual photograph. When they were first photographed it was without uniform but as the years wore on and the fire brigade took shape so the uniforms arrived. Eventually Mayson was photographing them as they stood smartly to attention alongside their own fire appliance. Every year Mayson also photographed the two-week Keswick Interdenominational Religious Convention which drew huge crowds to the town in July and gave him the chance to sell hundreds of photographs. He also befriended Millican Dalton, self-styled Professor of Adventure and took many pictures of the idiosyncratic old man.

Mayson was a handsome man with a slightly greying moustache and in his youth usually sported a large fashionable stetson, which made him look more like an American cowboy than a country photographer. In later life he was generally regarded as a slightly eccentric old man who always cycled to work from his home at Dubwath, near Bassenthwaite no matter what the weather. He was impatient and at times erratic. Legend has it that when he arrived at the level crossing on his way home one evening and found the barrier down, he turned around and cycled three miles out of his way to cross via a bridge rather than wait five minutes for the train to pass. His shop was said to be a den of dust and chaos and when the auctioneers arrived to clear it out years after his death, it proved a bothersome business. Yet here beneath the mess was a social history of photography. Thousands of postcards, glass plate negatives and old mahogany cameras went for a song. Even the sign for his model was still there, a century after it had been so painstakingly designed and painted. The business went under the hammer and was auctioned off in a hundred different directions.

Born and bred at Keswick Mayson's family could be traced back to the sixteenth century and he added to the lineage with five children of his own — three sons and two daughters, four of whom joined him in the business. He had married a Bessie Sanderson who was a distant relative by marriage and they settled in a house he had built for her at Dubwath. Their eldest child, Ralph, also took up photography and became a rock climber of some note. Bertram and his youngest sister Phyllis helped in the studio from the age of ten, colouring in the photographs while Horace who had suffered severe shell shock during the First World War was usually to be found at the back of the shop. When Henry Mayson died it was his daughter Phyllis, always known as Miss Mayson, who was to continue running the studio until old age forced her into retirement and brought a sad end to the family business in Lake Road.

Henry Mayson was an early master at the art of doctoring photographs. It was all part of the rivalry and the need to produce more striking photographs for the picture postcard industry. These shafts of light mysteriously appearing over Wastwater add a more dramatic effect to his picture as does the reflection on the Lake.

Another fine example of tampering where the background mountains have been made to look more dramatic. These are the Langdale Pikes but suddenly heightened with a careful brush of paint, courtesy of photographer and one-time artist Henry Mayson.

'A shepherd and his son went forth . . . to seek a straggler of their flock.' (Wordsworth)
Two shepherds, father and son, clutch their prize lambs.

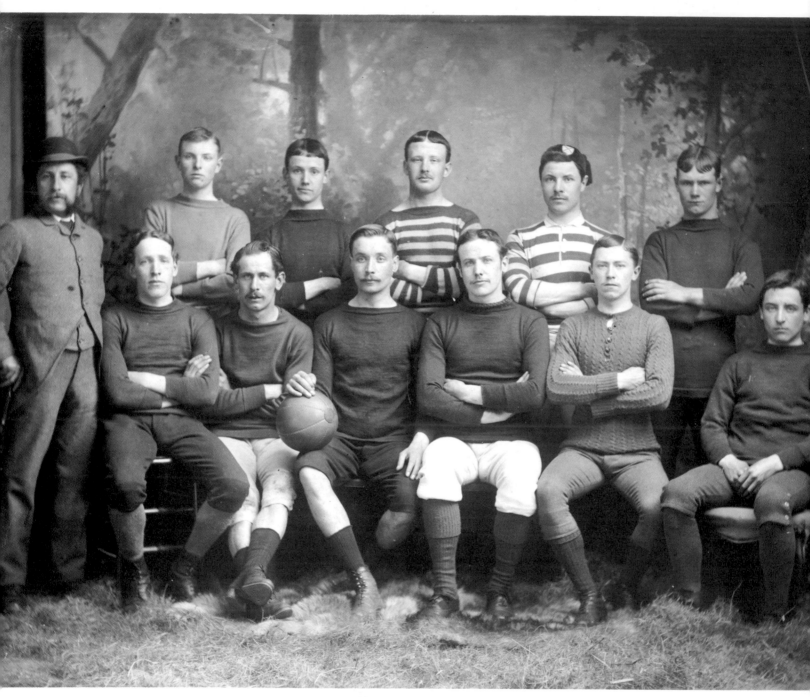

By 1890 sportsmen were becoming keen on having their photograph taken. This is the local Keswick football team and almost certainly one of the first footballing photographs to come out of the Lakes.

Mayson was not only a photographer but the licensee for fishing permits. This meant customers called into his shop to purchase a permit in the morning and then had their photograph taken when they returned. And their catches did not come much larger than this splendid salmon caught by Mr Coulthard.

A Royal visitor to Keswick. Princess Mary Louise arrives in the town centre, September 1902. Leaning out of the window on the left with a camera is George Abraham, one of Mayson's greatest rivals.

The Keswick Volunteer Fire Brigade. Every year the brigade visited Mayson's studio for their annual group picture. Initially their uniforms were a ragged assortment but eventually they would acquire a smart tunic and a fire appliance of their own.

'All shod with steel, We hiss'd along the polish'd ice.' (Wordsworth)
Skating on the River Greta in Keswick frozen over during the horrendous winter of 1895, plus a game of curling.

Millican Dalton, the self-styled Professor of Adventure was one of Lakeland's great eccentrics. A one-time insurance clerk, he turned his back on London and returned to the Lakes setting up home in a cave and living off the land. It didn't seem to do him any harm — he lived until he was eighty.

The old and the new. A crowd gathers at the Pheasant Hotel, near Bassenthwaite Lake, to inspect the arrival of the car.

A wedding in Keswick. Group photographs and particularly weddings were a necessary, and vital, part of the photographer's business. And what hats!

Alfred Pettitt

Alfred Pettitt was the father of Lakeland photography. Yet he began life not as a photographer but as an artist, opening up a gallery in Grasmere during 1853. He had come to the Lakes in 1851 from his home in Birmingham, settling initially in Windermere but moving shortly afterwards to Grasmere where he opened a gallery with his brother. It was an obvious spot for the Pettitts to choose, peaceful, picturesque and welcoming, and the two artists soon found a brisk trade around their small gallery. They were even visited by the Prince of Wales, later to become King Edward VII, when he toured Grasmere in 1857 and the young prince left clutching a small canvas by Alfred which no doubt hangs in some royal residence even to this day. It was a sale which would prove useful in later years as Pettitt advertised his gallery 'Patron HRH The Prince of Wales'.

Pettitt was probably introduced to photography by William Baldry the former schoolmaster at Grasmere who had opened a stationery shop in the village in 1856. Baldry was an early convert to photography and the Pettitts soon realised its importance. Before long they were displaying photographs in their gallery alongside their oil paintings and watercolours.

In 1858 the two Pettitts decided to move to larger premises in St John's Street, Keswick where they could extend their range of paintings and drawings to include even more photographs. It was a natural progression and Keswick was the obvious spot to ply this trade. Grasmere was still a small hamlet visited by pilgrims to Wordsworth's grave but with little potential for selling photographs especially when William Baldry had a shop almost totally devoted to photography. It was not even on the rail network, nor were there any plans to extend the rail link from Windermere whereas plans were well in hand for a railway to run between Keswick and Penrith. Keswick was also much larger with a population of 3,000 and had not yet been infiltrated by the photographic pioneers.

It was not long before Pettitt's gallery had become a major tourist attraction in itself. There was little else in the way of indoor amusement in Keswick so that when it rained, as it inevitably did, Pettitt's gallery was a centre for the rain-escaping visitor. The gallery was designed by Sir Alfred Waterhouse with what was described at the time as 'admirable taste'. Visitors called in to view the paintings and were soon entranced by the new world of photography. His paintings were not generally for sale, except those by his daughter Lucie but photographic prints of the many similar fine views around Keswick could be purchased. The cost was also in reach of most admirers unlike paintings which would have been considerably more expensive. And most tourists at this time were comfortable middle class professionals who could well afford the new innovation. The boom that would draw multitudes of working men and women to the Lakes on day excursions would not arrive until the turn of the century.

Inside Pettitt's gallery were three salons each packed with photographs, oil paintings and water colours of the Lake District. At the rear of the gallery was Pettitt's studio where tourists could sit and pose for their family portrait, an ideal souvenir of their stay in the Lakes and one which the children no doubt found equally fascinating. It was not long before Pettitt's gallery featured in the various guidebooks to the Lakes. In addition to selling cheap postcards Pettitt also advertised enlargements in black and white, monochrome, and group photographs of weddings, tennis and garden parties although the latter were by appointment only. When Pettitt began his only competition came from Joseph Flintoft and his famous model of the Lakes which could be seen at the Town Hall. But you had to pay to visit that whereas entrance to Pettitt's gallery was free of charge and open from eight in the morning until seven at night when the gas lamps would be lit to reveal an Aladdin's cave of photographic and artistic treasures.

Alfred Pettitt's fame quickly spread. He was befriended by Fox Talbot, the celebrated pioneering photographer and was soon displaying his work at exhibitions throughout the country where he won numerous medals. Many of these prize-winning photographs were published in 1870 in an album of scenic views entitled *Prize Photographs*. These incuded a selection of studies of Thirlmere Valley some years before it was flooded by Manchester Corporation and which are now of some historical importance. In 1878, shortly before his death he also completed a set of paintings of Thirlmere which were sold to Manchester Corporation for display in the Town Hall.

But Pettitt was not one to be content with snapping pretty views around Keswick. As rivalry intensified, so his approach varied. He took to the mountains, lugging his heavy equipment to the highest peaks, including Helvellyn and Skiddaw, in order to outdo his rivals with more dramatic shots. By this time he had engaged a young apprentice by the name of George Perry Abraham who no doubt encouraged his adventures on the mountains. In the years to come Abraham and his sons would be among the first photographers to specialise in mountain photography.

Pettitt died in March 1880. During the latter years of his life he had returned to his first love — painting — leaving his son to concentrate on the photography business. In his obituaries he is credited for his paintings rather than his photographs which is perhaps understandable given the attitude of many towards photography in those days. Art was considered a skill, whereas photography was thought to be a technique. Ruskin who had first seen photography in Venice in 1841 welcomed the new innovation and even dabbled in it himself whereas Turner lamented its arrival, dolefully forecasting the nadir of painting. It is ironic that Pettitt's paintings today fetch little more than £100 per canvas whereas just a couple of his thousands of glass plate negatives would fetch almost as much. Sadly few survive.

Pettitt brought an artist's eye to photography when it was still in its infancy. He understood light and shade and whereas most photographers were interested in technique he was interested in composition. Many of his photographs resemble Victorian watercolours, naturalistic but with a hint of romanticism where countryfolk ply their daily trade. Look at the Victorian paintings in any art gallery and you will see the same images Pettitt reproduced in his photographs. He may not have been the first to take photographs in the Lakes (the earliest known record is 1852) but he was certainly the first to realise its potential and to exploit it commercially. And this in turn inspired others to adopt the innovation.

Pettitt was one of the earliest innovators. Tilt the camera a little and you get a far more dramatic effect. This coach and horses carrying tourists over the Honister Pass looks to be descending at a far steeper angle.

Pettitt's favourite view. Thirlmere from the south, taken around 1875, some fifteen years before the flooding of the valley and the construction of the reservoir to serve Manchester. Much of the foreground is now under water.

The tiny church at Wythburn which dates back to 1640, on the east bank of Thirlmere. It still stands although the Nag's Head Inn which was once opposite has long been flooded.

Prawners at Grange-Over-Sands. A typical Pettitt postcard although Grange was well out of his territory. The boats tended to be used more for carrying visitors from Morecambe and for trips around the bay than for fishing.

The Bridge House at Ambleside dates back to the seventeenth century and is still a popular tourist attraction.

Edward Sankey

Barrow may not be able to boast the picturesque fells and bubbling becks of the nearby Lakes but it does have ships, and is, rightly, just as proud of them. For well over a century the town has been the industrial wing of the Lake District. Since 1840 when an ironworks opened using local ore in its smelters the town has been associated with iron and steel construction. Here the Vickers shipyard has been building ships, and in particular warships, for the world's navies since the 1870s so that many of the nation's great men-of-war have careered down its slipways and into the Walney Channel before venturing out onto the oceans.

Over the years the launching and fitting out of these mighty ships would prove a valuable source of material for one photographer, Edward Sankey. Today his bulging archive of photographs which span the Victorian and Edwardian eras of the town are a maritime historian's dream. Ships of every size and shape are to be found in his portfolio from the earliest mini-submarines to luxurious Atlantic voyaging liners, from the first primitive airships to bulbous-bowed oil tankers, from workaday trawlers to the grandest battleships of the Russian Imperial Navy. Whenever there was a launch, Sankey was there, his tripod erected alongside the official party or down on the slipway where he could capture the drama, recording the event either for a national newspaper or for reproduction as a postcard.

Edward Sankey began taking photographs during the 1890s and set up his own photography business in Barrow as Queen Victoria's long reign entered its final years. This was a time when iron hulls were replacing wooden ships and steam was supplanting sail, when Vickers employed more than 20,000 men and shipbuilding was one of the largest industries in the land. With the coming of steam and iron the world's navies began to expand rapidly and Sankey was on hand to chart their growth.

He began his working career as a printer on one of the local Barrow newspapers and had then formed his own small company. He quickly realised that his growing interest in photography and printing could easily be combined to provide a reasonably lucrative business. The picture postcard industry was also booming and although industrial Barrow may not have seemed the obvious venue for such trade, Sankey quickly realised its potential. What could be more exciting than the sight of these splendid vessels as they slid dramatically down the slipway or lay peacefully at anchor preparing to sail. He had a ready made market in newspapers, shipowners and, of course, the general public who could not help but be impressed by these mighty feats of engineering.

On important launch days when there was often a Royal visitor, half the town would wend its way down the Michaelson Road towards the Vickers yard to watch the freshly painted ship plunge into the river. Schoolchildren generally enjoyed a half-day holiday and wives would join their husbands in the crowd alongside the ship. To the traditional accompaniment of a brass band the youngsters would loudly cheer the new vessel on its way. And somewhere near the front of the launch platform or beneath the ship's towering hull Edward Sankey could usually be found perched behind his camera and tripod. Within hours of the launch Sankey would have developed his glass plates and run off hundreds of postcards which would then be quickly distributed and sold around the town as a fitting souvenir of a memorable day.

Sankey's first and, in hindsight, possibly his greatest scoop came in 1911 when Vickers launched the first naval airship. The company telegraphed him with the day and time of the launch and Sankey was waiting prepared with his camera. That alone might have been an historic moment but within minutes of its launch, Airship Number One, better known as *Mayfly*, foundered and broke its back in Cavendish dock. It was the end of *Mayfly* and Sankey had captured the drama forever on glass plate.

But there were other memorable pictures, especially that of the Japanese cruiser, *Kongo* which was launched on May 18th 1912. One of three Japanese warships built at Barrow, *Kongo* was 704 feet long with a beam of 91 feet and carried a crew of over 1,100 men. It was a stunning spectacle that drew large crowds to the town and within hours of its midday launch Sankey had reproduced postcards for sale to the general public. Such was the interest in *Kongo* that by the end of the day he had sold more than a thousand postcards. Thirty years later *Kongo* was still ploughing the oceans but was finally sunk off Formosa during the Second World War by a United States submarine.

Again Sankey was on hand as one of Vickers' earliest submarines, *A2*, crept out of its mooring, and ventured up the Furness in April 1903 to considerable curiosity. The small flimsy craft weighing just 204 tonnes and carrying only a handful of crew members survived until 1920 and helped forge a long relationship with submarines at Vickers that would culminate many years later in the awesome nuclear submarines of the Trident and Polaris classes. In 1907 the armour cruiser *Rurik* was launched for the Imperial Russian Navy and two years later Sankey photographed the Brazilian Navy's *Sao Paulo* and HMS *Vanguard* side by side in Buccleuch dock. Rarely can that dock have boasted two such magnificent battleships. In 1917 *Vanguard* would be sunk at Scapa Flow with only two survivors from its 850 crew.

Much of Sankey's early work was carried out on board the Furness Railways' two steamships *Lady Moira* and *Lady Evelyn* which ploughed the daily route between Fleetwood and Barrow. The ships would leave Barrow at 9 a.m. with Edward Sankey and his camera on board, arriving at Fleetwood in just over the hour. They would then depart from Fleetwood at 10.30 overflowing with holidaymakers from nearby Blackpool. By midday they would be back in Barrow where they would be met by a stream of coaches and trains to carry them into the heart of the Lake District. Sankey would have spent his time on board ship taking photographs of the passengers and would then rush back to his shop to develop the pictures. When the passengers returned to Barrow for the 6.30 p.m. crossing Sankey would be there to deliver the results. It was a lucrative little sideline.

This was Sankey's one concession to portrait photography. Unlike so many of the Victorian photographers, he cared little for posed family portraits or wedding groups. He was a freelancer, possibly the earliest in the Lake District or even the North of England, who would sell to newspapers, magazines or companies. Sankey had no studio, just a shop where he developed and printed his postcards. Although Barrow and its ships formed a large proportion of his output, the bulk came from his Lakeland travels. Sankey was undoubtedly one of the most commercial of the Lakeland photographers travelling miles between Cockermouth and Keswick in the north to Kendal and Barrow in the south focussing on landscapes which would eventually be turned into thousands of postcards for the summer trade. And besides the popular landscapes there are countless pictures of peddlers, Victorian holidaymakers at Walney Beach, and of course nearby Furness Abbey, the magnificent crumbling edifice that had been founded by King Stephen in 1127.

Besides his shipbuilding photographs Sankey was also official photographer to the Furness Railway Company, a post that gave him the opportunity not just to indulge in some superb shots of the Lakeland railways but found him on call whenever there was a train crash. A midnight message and he would be on his way to wherever the crash had occurred preparing to take the official photographs for the inquiry. And when he was not performing that function he might turn up at any of the local Lakeland stations to photograph the staff for their annual portrait. Even the smaller stations would employ as many as twenty men. Like the ships, his railway photographs have also provided a rich archive for the historian. There are trains whistling over the Kent viaduct or steaming up Lakeland valleys as well as overturned tank engines and wrecked carriages. Here was the romance of steam at its most romantic in an age now long past.

In 1924 Sankey was joined in the business by his eldest son Raymond. Together they continued to take photographs well into Edward's late life. When Edward Sankey died during the 1960s aged 90, he had left behind an archive of more than 10,000 photographs many of them on glass plate. Today they constitute a fascinating alternative view of the Lakes where the ingenuity and brawn of man takes precedence over the romance of the countryside.

The Barrow photographer Edward Sankey is best remembered for his photographs in and around the Vickers Shipyard. This was probably his greatest scoop, the launch of Naval Airship Number 1, better known as Mayfly, *which promptly broke its back in Cavendish Dock.*

The Japanese Battleship Kongo *being fitted out at Vickers during 1913. His photographs of the spectacular* Kongo*, one of the largest warships in the world, sold in their thousands.* Kongo *was finally sunk off Formosa by a US submarine during the Second World War.*

The Michaelson Road and entrance to Vickers. At one time the shipyard employed 20,000 workers.

'Here we go, here we go!' The Furness Railway steamer, Walney *carrying football supporters from Barrow to Fleetwood, probably for a match at Blackpool. Sankey would regularly sail with the steamers taking photographs of the passengers on the way out and then delivering the finished product on the way back later that day.*

An early Vickers submarine, known as A2. Built in 1903 the submarine carried just a handful of crew members but survived until 1920.

Devonshire Dock, 1907. Being fitted out are Rurik, an armoured cruiser for the Russian Imperial Navy and HMS Natal for the Royal Navy.

A Bank Holiday crowd on Walney Beach, 1907.

Washing day in old Barrow during the 1890s.

One of Sankey's jobs for the Furness Railway Company was to take photographs of train crashes. This particular crash was at Millom.

Although many of Sankey's photographs have an industrial edge to them he could also be artistic as in this fine example of a train steaming across the Kent viaduct.

Lakeland Peddler at Newby Bridge, 1908.

As well as ships Sankey was the official photographer for the Furness Railway Company. This was the staff at Ulverston station.

A Stone Breaker in a quarry near Greenodd. When Sankey did venture into the Lakes he took his industrial background with him. He may have taken many landscapes but his finest pictures always involved people, workers and engineering.

Sam Thompson

Sam Thompson was a genuine amateur. He was not a professional photographer who earned his living by the camera but someone for whom photography was a hobby which just happened to coincide conveniently with his other interests, walking and cycling. On most weekends, especially during the long summer days or at Bank Holidays, Thompson could be spotted, hobnail boots, waterproof and trilby, striding out across the Fells, his camera and tripod nodding up and down on his back as he steadily climbed the roughshod paths towards the summit. He usually travelled alone, preferring his own company to that of the crowd though he was always amiable enough and ready to pass a moment's conversation with some other rambler. In the evening he might stop overnight at some small hilltop inn, or be recognised dashing to catch the last train home.

Thompson was born and bred in the Red Rose capital of Lancaster. Here among the alleyways and cobbled streets that surrounded Roger of Poitou's formidable castle where Robert the Bruce had pillaged and burned, he would stalk with his camera, focusing on crumbling ancient buildings or relics of the city's distant past. Once the proud stronghold of John of Gaunt and the Lancastrians, Lancaster by the time of Thompson's birth in 1871, was a city struggling to rediscover its earlier fortunes. The ships that had carried mahogany, tobacco and sugar from the Indies had now been left high and dry as the Lune silted up. The moorings and warehouses stood deserted and empty but by the end of the nineteenth century Lancaster would have moved into a second renaissance, manufacturing linoleum and oilcloth. As the young Thompson wandered its streets Lancaster must have seemed a city of rich history but little future.

He was born the eldest son of Mr and Mrs Adam Thompson, well known farmers of Scotforth on the outskirts of the city, and would spend his entire life within a mile of his birthplace. He rarely travelled venturing only to the Lakes in the North, the Trough of Bowland in the south, Morecambe Bay to the west or the Dales to the East. And who could blame him when a morning's bike ride or a cheap rail excursion could take him into some of the finest hill walking country this side of the Alps. For a man who loved the country he could hardly have chosen a finer spot to be born.

He first took to photography as a young man and was taking photographs by 1890 after realising that he could combine the activity with his love of walking and cycling. He was not a poor man and could well afford the equipment even though it perhaps meant forsaking some other pleasure. Before long he would be strapping camera and tripod to the iron frame of his cycle and heading precariously down the road towards Lancaster station to catch a train up to the Lakes or cycling off down country lanes and into the Wyre Valley. A 4s 6d (22½p) third class return would take him into the heart of Lakeland and there he was free to roam or cycle its quiet backwaters. Next to walking there was no finer way to see the Lakes than from the saddle of a bicycle and at any time the bike could be discarded, propped up safely against a stone wall, while he took off over the fells with his camera.

He was a man of the country, could talk the language of countryfolk and understood their ways and superstitions. He would chat for hours with woodsmen, gamekeepers, smithies or cowhands, patiently waiting for them to pose before his camera. Even Romany gipsies found their way into his album, sometimes sitting around woodsmoking campfires, cooking, drying clothes or playfully laughing into his camera. The results were superb. Ageing men, three generations old, born before Waterloo; country squires conferring over their game stocks; weatherbeaten faces, and fishermen boasting their catch or casting their favourite flies. Haymakers at tea, village smithies bending before flying sparks, and soft wintry snow scenes.

Some of his finest images were captured out at Sunderland Point where he photographed the fishermen and trawlermen who plied their trade from the small Lancastrian port. The fishermen in their guernsey sweaters and sou'-westers posed happily for Thompson in a series of portraits that rank with any of those taken by the better known Herbert Sutcliffe of Whitby. At Sunderland Point he befriended John Walker, another outstanding amateur photographer who despite his early wealth died in poverty in a Lancaster Work House in 1939. Perhaps Thompson did create a sentimental image that carefully hid the reality of life in the country but it contrasted with the dingy backyards, dark alleyways and squalid almshouses that he often portrayed in Lancaster. His pictures are a statement and the message is clear; life in the country has a nobility that the town cannot rival.

In Keswick Thompson met the Abraham Brothers and joined them on one of their climbs. He watched them photographing the crags with tweed-suited climbers clinging dangerously to the rockface and decided to try his hand at a spot of mountain photography. The results may not have been as spectacular as the Abrahams', lacking their drama and impact but the technical quality was just as good. Here was a generation of pioneers climbing in shirtsleeves, braces and trilbies on spring afternoons where today goretex, pitons and crash helmets have pride of place. He soon became a close friend of the Abrahams and joined them on many a dashing adventure up the mountains. But he was never as graceful or as adept a climber and mostly his exploits were confined to the lower reaches and the easier grade climbs. He was happy simply to set foot on the crags and to then let his camera do the rest. One of his finest pictures was a self portrait looking across towards the icy gullies and snow peaks of Red Screes, his tripod neatly perched on some rocky knoll with his hand ready and poised to squeeze the cable release.

Thompson's photographs were soon on show throughout Britain. He won prizes at Leeds, Manchester and Edinburgh and exhibited at the Royal Photographic Society in London regularly during the 1930s. He was active in the Morecambe, Heysham and District Photography Society and for much of his life was the backbone of his own Lancaster Photographic Society. During the War some of his prints toured America and Canada as part of a Royal Photographic Society selection of the best British pictures. It was a great honour, especially for one who was still an amateur, receiving only the occasional payment for a picture reprinted in a magazine or newspaper. It was his proudest achievement.

Because he was an amateur Thompson was not in the business of studio portraits, weddings, postcards, photogravures and so forth. He may have sold the odd landscapes to the woollen industry but in the main he did not have to trek around trying to better his rivals in order to survive commercially. He could take his time, go where he pleased, use whatever camera he wished. That helped him focus on the nature of his work and the quality of his pictures. If he did not like a particular photograph he could discard it, unlike the commercial photographers who had to live by the results of their work. Nor did he have to waste time going out in search of work or wait patiently behind a counter for the work to arrive. He was a free agent. It meant that his only criteria was quality.

For most of his life Thompson worked for the Rembrandt Intaglio Company in Queen Street mill where he settled for a steady nine to five routine that left him ample time to pursue his hobby. He never married and lived with his brother and two sisters at Scotforth until his death in March 1945. He had been out walking, caught a cold and pneumonia set in. Within days he died at the Royal Infirmary in Lancaster. He was 74.

A short, erect figure with sharp features, penetrating eyes and a walrus moustache Thompson had proved that you do not have to be a full-time professional to produce a quality picture. The amateur can just as easily take an expert shot. Provided you have the technical skill, what then matters is the artistic eye. Thompson clearly demonstrated that talent in his portfolio which almost certainly came from his love of the country. Once asked what he enjoyed most in life he replied, 'a country life, a walk or a cycle ride with my camera'. It was a fitting epitaph.

Many of Thompson's finest photographs were taken at Sunderland Point where he quickly became friendly with the various fishermen who soon became the subjects for some of his most celebrated portraits.

Thompson knew the Abraham Brothers well and although he was not as expert a climber himself he loved the mountains and carried his camera with him whenever he ventured onto the crags.

The cobbled streets and back alleys of Lancaster were a photographer's delight and Thompson's many pictures have left a rich record of the social conditions in the Lancashire city shortly after the turn of the century.

Life in the city was just as hard as that in the country. Conditions were miserable and often unhygienic. Few houses had running water and hot water was a luxury. If you wanted water it meant a trip outside to fill the bucket.

Winters could be just as savage in Lancaster as in the Lakes, especially when the River Lune froze leaving ships stranded on the icy banks and snowbound dockside.

It was not unusual to see genuine Romany gipsies wandering the Lakes or Wyre Valley and Thompson was well known to many of them.

Thompson was an outstanding amateur photographer whose portraits of countryfolk and fishermen deserve to be a part of any Lakeland portfolio. This is a gamekeeper in the Wyre Valley and (opposite) a woodsman pauses to light his clay pipe.

A Lancaster beggar.

Elevenses during haymaking. A gentle reminder of England in another era.

Charles Walmsley

Charles E. Walmsley was a son of the Lakes who understood and captured its subtleties in as fine a series of landscapes as any photographer. He was born in Ambleside in 1862 and save for a few years spent at Hartsop on the far edge of the Kirkstone Pass, lived there his entire life in the family home at Prospect Cottage. He was not a pioneer, nor was he an innovator; he did not scramble up mountaintops, nor did he risk life and limb for the perfect shot. Rather he was a simple cameraman who trod the fells and villages in search of Lakeland life and the delicate shades of its landscape.

Photography was already half a generation old when Walmsley joined the studio of Moses Bowness in Ambleside. Bowness had been practising his art since around 1865 at Gale View in Ambleside and was a well established figure when Walmsley first knocked on his door. The young Walmsley had taken to photography in his youth and was an equally keen and accomplished artist. Perhaps it was his love of oil painting which gave him such an insight into photography. He was always peering through Bowness' cluttered shop window and when the old man offered him an apprenticeship it was like a gift from heaven. But life in this studio turned out not to be altogether to the liking of the young man. Bowness was a portrait and group photographer, concentrating on this commercial side of the business and had little interest in the more artistic world of landscape photography.

Ambleside, where once the Romans had pitched their tents, stood on a hillside above the murmuring Rothay, just a short dash from Lake Windermere. Here Dr Arnold of Rugby School had once lived and the writer Harriet Martineau, while William Wordsworth when Distributor of Stamps occupied an office in the town. By the late 1870s Ambleside, population 2,000, was beginning to flourish as a Lakeland tourist centre. Although there was no rail connection there were three or four coaches a day arriving from Windermere station bound for Keswick in the north. Three largish hotels and plenty of lodging houses testified to the growing popularity of the spot while all the new guidebooks recommended it as a useful springing off post for the southern lakes. The twisting cobbled streets with their rough grey stone buildings, back alleys and floral decorations made Ambleside a more pleasant prospect than the rather grand and formal centre at Windermere or even distant Keswick where the wind blows mournfully around Skiddaw and Blencathra. Yet without a rail link it would always remain a slightly more remote, distant attraction that would not change until the coming of the car.

Ambleside suited Walmsley well but Messrs Bowness did not. Walmsley was not a studio photographer although he did take many fine portraits but they belong to the outdoors, in their natural settings. Ushering noisy tourists and the spoilt wailing children of the wealthy into the back studio was not his idea of photography. By 1894 Charles had persuaded his brother James to go into partnership with him and together they purchased premises in Rydal Road, Ambleside and set up their own small business. It was to be an enormous success. Walmsley was now freed of the constraints of Messrs Bowness and could pursue his own interests without worry. He still took many studio portraits which after all were a lucrative and dependable source of income but it was no longer the only aspect of his work. James could concentrate on the day-to-day running of the business while Charles was turning more and more towards the outdoors and as techniques developed, so Walmsley seized the commercial potential.

Adopting photogravure, a process whereby a photographic image is formed on a metal plate using a series of tiny holes, Walmsley was able to reproduce thousands of prints cheaply and quickly. It opened up a whole new market for him. His prints could be purchased in small Lakeland gift shops or in the large departmental stores of the big cities. Before long his landscapes could be spotted on walls and in studies throughout the world. American President Woodrow Wilson had a wall of his White House residence devoted entirely to Walmsley photographs and would take great delight in showing visiting dignitaries and statesmen his Walmsley collection.

The most famous of these photogravures was the Shepherd which reached corners of the world as remote from the Lake District as imaginable. It was spotted hanging in a woodsman's shack in British Guiana and in a squatter's hut in a remote valley of Canada. Walmsley had probably done more to popularise an image of the Lakes than any other man of his generation. Thousands of his bromide prints were sold throughout the world, particularly in America where the President's interest seemed to spark off even greater sales. He won prizes wherever he exhibited, especially in America, and his Shepherd photograph was so popular that it was insured for £1,000. There were other memorable pictures such as his bracken harvest, yachts tilting gracefully on Windermere and charcoal burners sitting around their smouldering embers.

Walmsley was a quiet, refined man of gentle disposition. Smart, slightly formal though with a friendly smile. He was also deeply religious, a devoted Methodist as well as a member of the local Band of Hope and the Choral Society. He was a keen angler who liked nothing better than to put aside his camera, pick up his favourite rod and cast a fly from a boat on Brotherswater. He knew every stream and backwater in the Lakes and had fished most of them. Like so many of his generation and class, he was a well read man, as knowledgeable as any on Wordsworth and the literary associations of the Lakes, and his library contained many rare editions. He contributed to various newspapers and magazines, not just photographs but articles as well, particularly the *Lake District Herald*, and his photographs were used to illustrate books throughout the world.

A tall and spare figure he was unmistakable on the fells with his camera and bags strapped firmly to his back. In rain or sunshine Walmsley could be spotted perched by a Lake pool or standing on a crag, his equipment unfolded, tripod angled, awaiting the moment when the light would best suit his shot. He retired in 1929 and died twelve years later in March 1941, aged 79, at Prospect Cottage after a short illness.

Walmsley knew and understood the folklore of the Lakes and was a respected and known figure wherever he trod. Charles Dixon, the craggy shepherd he had made so famous with his renowned photograph was typical of the characters Walmsley befriended in his search for the soul of the Lakes. If ever a single photograph captured the heart of Victorian Lakeland then it was Charles Dixon astride his white horse on the fells gently carrying an injured sheep back to the fold.

Many of Walmsley's photographs were reproduced using the photogravure process and sold cheaply to tourists. Some are even said to have hung in President Woodrow Wilson's White House. This was a particular favourite with the public.

'Emerging from the silvery vapours, lo! A Shepherd and his Dog!' (Wordsworth)
Another typical Walmsley picture evoking Lakeland life: the shepherd with his dogs and sheep.

'Smooth life had Flock and Shepherd in old time.' (Wordsworth)
Rounding up the sheep on the fells.

Walmsley probably captured the mood of the Lakes more than any other photographer, especially in this picture of the sheep being fed as dusk fell.

Collecting the bracken.

Although Walmsley had little interest in studio photography he took many superb outdoor portraits, particularly of the farmers, shepherds and farmhands he stumbled upon during his travels.

Walmsley was often to be seen wandering the fells with his camera strapped to his back in search of a fresh angle. On this occasion he stumbled across a scene somewhat less than rural as the chauffeur performed his duty.

Yachts dipping in the breeze on Windermere.

An idyllic Lakeland scene as captured by Charles Walmsley.

Photo credits

The author is most grateful to the following for supplying photographs used in this book.

Abbot Hall Museum, Kendal, pages 10, 16, 19, 21 (bottom right), 23, 24, 29, 30, 40-42, 50-59, 65-68, 71, 137, 139; Armitt Trust, pages 60-62, 134-135; Reg Dixon, pages 43-47; Fell and Rock Climbing Club, pages 12, 13, 27, 28, 31-37; Fenty Collection, pages 11, 69-70; George Holt, pages 90-94; Kendal Library, page 72; Lancaster Library, pages 118-131; John Marsh, pages 98-101; Robin Pembridge, pages 85-87, 89, 95; Raymond Sankey, pages 104-115; Helena Thompson Museum, Workington, pages 75-82; Victoria and Albert Museum and Frederick Warne, page 22; Whitehaven Museum, pages 20 and 21 (3 left hand photos); Windermere Library, pages 17 and 18.